The Elder Scrolls®
─── ONLINE ───

THE OFFICIAL SURVIVAL
GUIDE TO TAMRIEL

The Elder Scrolls®

— ONLINE —

The Official Survival Guide to Tamriel

Tori Schafer

Titan Books

London

An Insight Editions Book

CONTENTS

Introduction..................9
Skyrim......................11
  The Proper Supplies
  Clash with the Cold
  Meeting a Bear
  Conclusion

Hammerfell..................27
  Surviving the Heat
  Sea Travel
  Wound Care
  Conclusion

Elsweyr.....................43
  Be Wary of Thieves
  Surviving an Abduction
  How to Survive a Plunge from a Waterfall
  A Guide to Furstocks
  Conclusion

Black Marsh 59
  Dangers of the Marsh
  Black Marsh Wildlife
  What Are the Hist?
  Conclusion

Morrowind...................77
  The Great Houses
  Avoiding (Legal) Assassinations
  Volcano Safety
  The Tribunal
  Conclusion

Cyrodiil 91

High Rock 93
    Finding Your Direction
    Horse Riding
    The Orcs
    Conclusion

Valenwood 115
    The Green Pact
    Meat on the Menu
    Water Worries
    Conclusion

Summerset Isle 131
    Magic and Mages
    Recovering from Magical Attacks
    The Fundamentals of Camping
    Conclusion

The Daedric Planes 149
    A Primer on Daedric Princes
    Daedric Cults
    Conclusion

Farewell and Safe Travels . . 167

About the Author 168
About the Illustrator 168

A NOTE FROM THE AUTHOR

It has been said that the eyes dine on words but feast on pictures, and Ja'dasha has never been one to set a poor table. To that end, this one has made certain that her survival guide is rich with imagery. The images reproduced in these pages were acquired and commissioned by generous Ja'dasha at great expense, and in some cases with great difficulty and no small amount of personal risk. It is best for all concerned that Ja'dasha not divulge the full provenance of every picture you see between the covers of this book. Simply consider them a gift from Ja'dasha to help prepare you for the magnificent and terrible sights you will see as you travel the length Tamriel. You are welcome.

INTRODUCTION

Ja'dasha's father always told her that scholars are like an awning on a cloudy day: unheeded and unneeded until the rains begin to pour. And while this one is no scholar, she has learned much over the years: how to survive blinding blizzards, how to make your way through the desert's heat, and how to bind wounds and scavenge for meals. Such are the necessary skills for the Baandari, after all.

Tamriel is like a patchwork quilt. To the west lay deserts and crags. To the east are volcanoes and swamps. Islands, oases, jungles, and tundras … the nature of this land shifts more often than the phases of the moons, and so too shifts its dangers. This is why Ja'dasha's survival guide is so needed, and why your septims were well spent on this book. In these pages, this one will speak of the dangers that lurk in every corner of Tamriel, and how you can weather such threats on your travels.

A word of caution before we begin. There is little that can be done for those who shun all aid. Read carefully, yes, but also know that the greatest advice is simple: You are in trouble, walker? Seek help. Whether it be healers or knights, priests or merchants, always look toward others in your times of need. They will be your greatest assets, even greater than this magnificent book penned by the wise Ja'dasha. But if no help is near? If you are all alone? Then this survival guide may be all that stands between you and Sands Behind the Stars.

SKYRIM

The land of Skyrim is known for its snowy mountaintops and frigid climates. Even in the middle of summer you will find snow in these lands; Ja'dasha has seen this. The southern reaches host more mild temperatures and green forests, though even those comparatively lush places host bitter winters. To the north you shall face the Sea of Ghosts, filled with glaciers and icebergs. And wherever you travel in Skyrim you will find many caves and ruins, filled with Dwemer technology and bloodthirsty Falmer. The land's beauty is very much matched by its dangers.

The Nords of Skyrim are a people as unyielding as the land they live in. They are a proud group who face dangers every day, from caves filled with giant spiders to harrowing blizzards. This resolve is matched only by their merrymaking, for their celebration songs hold as much passion as their battle cries. You will find few races who are as quick to laugh as they are to rage. And the Nords prefer it that way.

Traveling safely through this land requires proper preparation, keen instinct, and the wisdom that lies within this guide. So have no worries, walker. The pages to come will teach you all you must know to face the threats of Skyrim.

THE PROPER SUPPLIES

Let us start our discussion by considering what to prepare before you take the first step of your journey. The proper supplies needed for any journey will vary depending on what land you are traversing. In these first splendid pages, Ja'dasha will cover the basic supplies specifically needed to journey through Skyrim. Any specific supplies needed for different lands will be covered in later chapters.

WATER AND FOOD

Only a fool would leave for a journey without first supplying themselves with water and food. So take into account how much you will need each day, and the number of days you plan to travel. Simple, no? The best food is that which will not spoil. This may take the form of such portable consumables as saltines, jerky, or nuts. If you are unsure how long your foodstuffs will last, consult one more experienced than you.

While some less traveled may be tempted to fill their packs with tasty delicacies like sweet rolls and mudcrab legs, it's far better to pack hearty, filling meals that are well preserved. Charred skeever meat, horker and ash yam stew, and mammoth cheese were staples for Ja'dasha during her journey in Skyrim. These provisions can be found in most towns and cities in the snowy kingdom.

For all of Skyrim's dangers, water will never be in short supply. The terrain features many lakes and rivers, and should the need arise you can always melt the snow. Some may be tempted to eat the snow directly, but this is a fool's choice. The snow's coldness will freeze your bones, leaving you thirstier than expected. The healers call this dehydration.

Depending on where you travel in Skyrim, options for hunting can be plentiful. Deer, rabbits, and other game may be your main source of food, should your own supplies run short. Hunting will take precious time and energy, however, and will delay your journey. So plan to hunt only if there is naught else to eat. Otherwise, it is best to conserve your energy and continue onward.

TOOLS AND OTHER ITEMS

Ja'dasha could write an entire book alone on tools and equipment you may need to bring with you while journeying in Tamriel. Perhaps one day she shall. For now, the fundamentals. Tents to keep you dry in the rain are a good start. A blanket or mat to sleep on will save you from lying on the frigid, muddy, or otherwise unpleasant ground. Flint can help you start a fire, and a knife can help with everything from building shelters to creating even more tools. Below, Ja'dasha lists the most useful tools for travelers to bring on their journey.

- **Torches**
  These will light your path in both the darkness of night and any caves you may be foolish enough to explore.

- **Sleeping mat**
  Especially important for colder lands, for a freezing ground makes for a freezing body. And let us not forget the comfort it affords.

- **Tents**
  The moons may be pleasant to look upon, but they are often hidden by rain clouds or snowfall. You will be more comfortable, warm, and protected within a tent. Flax and cotton tents are best, for these sturdy materials will protect you from rain while still being breathable during warm weather. Some wealthier travelers may be tempted by tents of spider silk or silverweave, but these make for poor cover, and tend to rip and tear after only a few weeks of use.

- **Flint and kindling**
  Unless your traveling party includes a mage, it is best to have flint available to start fires. Kindling may be easier to come by should you pass through wooded areas.

- **Extra clothing**
  Too many walkers choose to journey with just the simple shirt on their back. Should your clothes become wet or sullied—as they surely will—you will be grateful that you listened to the wise Ja'dasha on this matter. To this end, make sure that the clothes you pack are suitable for the hardships of travel. Though shadowhide may be too pricey for most, leather jerkins and boots can endure the harshest of journeys.

- **Rope**
  Whether you need to scale down a cliff or bundle your kindling, rope offers all manner of uses. Keep it dry, keep it close, and keep it away from idiots.

continued on next page

- **Waterskins**
  One of Ja'dasha's wisest purchases was her superb hide waterskin, which has seen her through thick and thin. Everyone in your party should keep their own waterskin, and keep it full whenever possible. Thirst will kill you quicker than starvation.

- **Map and compass**
  The map tells you to go north. The compass tells you which way is north. Should you have neither, prepare to be lost.

- **Sturdy pack**
  Where are all your supplies to go without a pack to carry them? Unsurprisingly, the sturdier the better. A pack will do you little good if it decides to tear midway through your journey.

Though these are the basic supplies one may journey with, this is by no means a complete list. What is most important is that you prepare for whatever lies ahead. This means studying the land where you will travel, and noting what tools may be useful.

CLASH WITH THE COLD

Listen to Ja'dasha: The winter in Skyrim? This is no joke, walker. Many who fail to take precautions have frozen to death atop some moons-forsaken mountaintop. Even we Khajiit, with our beautiful coats of fur, must prepare for the icy winds and endless snow. So too must you prepare before you travel, yes? Or you will not be traveling much afterward.

EXPOSURE TO THE ELEMENTS

For those who possess the arts of magic, warmth is as simple as casting a flame spell or protecting yourself with alteration magic. But most of us folk in Tamriel have no magic or mages to call upon during our travels. And so Ja'dasha will concentrate on the more mundane means of keeping oneself warm.

DRESS IN LAYERS

A single coat, no matter how thick, will not suffice. You will want to dress in layers of clothing should you encounter colder climates. A mage once told Ja'dasha that this is because air becomes trapped between the clothing layers. This one thought the mage mad, but perhaps there is some truth to it? This one has seen Khajiit with the thickest of winter coats shivering from the cold while Ja'dasha remained toasty within her many layers of cloth.

AVOID THE COLD

The cold of Skyrim will sap your strength faster than Ja'dasha downs a tankard of moon-sugar rum. It is in your best interest to prevent exposure to the elements and avoid the icy wind by covering as much of your skin as you can. If you wish to lie upon the ground, be sure to first lay down thick cloth. Avoid becoming wet, especially if you are prone to sweating. The wet walker is a dead walker in the unforgiving cold.

FALLING THROUGH ICE

The lakes of Skyrim can freeze during the colder months, and their vastness means that walking atop the ice can be far quicker than going around them. Traveling in such a way, however, presents the hazard of falling through the ice you walk upon. Struggle and panic, and you are likely to end up dead. Heed Ja'dasha's wisdom if you wish to survive.

- **Remain calm**
  The water will be icy enough to take your breath away and fill you with fear. Do not allow this to overwhelm you, for you will need to move quickly.

- **Do not struggle**
  You may try to pull off your heavy clothing, thinking it will pull you downward. Do not waste such time. Your clothes contain warm air that will pull you upward, helping you float to the surface.

- **Find strong ice**
  Once you have floated upward and found the hole you fell through, the time has come to pull yourself out. Try to find the direction you last walked before the ice broke, for this ice should be strong enough to support you.

- **Escape the water**
  This is easier said than done, and the freezing water will do little to help your strength. Place your arms on

continued on next page

the ice and begin to kick your legs, pushing your body forward. This will allow you to slide onto the ice like a horker.

- **Crawl forward**
  If you fell through the ice once, it is likely to happen again. Do not stand; distribute your weight evenly as you crawl forward. The best way to do this is to slide on your belly, again imitating a horker.

- **Warm yourself**
  Head toward land, start a fire, and change your clothes if possible. The water may not have killed you, but the cold temperature certainly will.

◆

FIND SHELTER

When you find your strength at its last, the time has come to rest away from the cold. Ja'dasha's preference, of course, is to find a warm tavern with a cozy fire to sit beside. From the Lonely Troll to the Withered Tree, there are many lovely establishments within Skyrim that you may visit during your travels. But what if you choose to travel away from the beaten path? Or, moons forbid, what if you have no coin left to pay for accommodations?

If there are no traditional lodgings to be found nearby, you must search for a nontraditional alternative. A cave would suit your purpose nicely, though there is no telling if you will find a frostbite spider nest inside. If you see no cave, or do not wish to risk such dangers, a small shelter can be made within the snow itself.

First you must find a safe place to create your temporary homestead, especially if you are traveling upon one of the many mountains of Skyrim. Be sure the location you select is not along the path of a potential avalanche. Check for broken trees and other debris at the bottom of any clearing you find. If you see such debris, then the side of the clearing is a far safer option. It is also best to avoid cliffs and high locations, yes? Better to not plummet to your death.

Search for a large drift piled high and dig a hollow, taller than it is wide. This will ensure that the structure does not fall upon your head. You must dig your shelter's entrance below the hollow that you make, so the wind does not find its way within. Create small holes atop your shelter so that you may breathe. The warmth will do you little good if there is no air to fill your lungs. It is also wise to strengthen your shelter with branches and other debris, should they be easy to obtain.

Any improvements to your shelter must be weighed against the effort it will take to create that improvement. It is best to work quickly and efficiently, for you cannot afford to exhaust yourself and begin to sweat. Such wetness beneath your clothing will drain you of what precious heat you have, exposing you further to the cold climate.

GREATER DANGERS

Being cold is never a pleasure, especially to us who walk upon the sands. But you need not be a healer to know that the frost can kill if you are not prepared to face it. Listen to Ja'dasha, for she will tell you how to survive such ordeals.

FROSTBITE

The cold of Skyrim is enough to freeze your flesh. This is known to healers as frostbite, a most apt name. Frostbite will first attack your fingers, toes, and tail before moving up along your limbs. Ja'dasha has seen entire hands overtaken by frostbite. It was not a pretty sight.

This bane will first present as pale and stiff skin, occasionally forming blisters. It is only when the affected flesh has been warmed that it turns red and purple. If you are unfortunate enough that your skin turns black, it means the flesh has died completely. Then it is time to either find a very skilled healer or a very sharp saw. The best way to combat frostbite, as with most wounds, is to never receive it. Dressing warmly and following Ja'dasha's other advice to stay warm will help this.

Should the worst come to pass, however, you should never rub the skin, nor rupture blisters that may have formed. Use whatever healing salve you have on the affected flesh and dress the limb loosely. This one has heard of a wondrous salve called aloe vera that is perfect for such situations. Elevate the limb if possible, and drink plenty of water. Last, and perhaps most importantly, you must get to a warm shelter. The less the severity of the freezing, the more likely the flesh can heal.

As you may suspect, a limb that has frozen must be thawed. This should only be done if you have found shelter, and are at no risk of the limb refreezing. The thawed skin will be soft and red, possibly even purple. If the skin turns black,

well…Ja'dasha has said this before: The limb will need to be cut from the rest of your body, for it has died (which is how this one's uncle earned the name "No-Tail" Ta'dashi). Keep applying the same healing methods of salves, loose bandages, elevation, and drinking plenty of water. Should the flesh not be dead, it will recover.

HYPOTHERMIA

Frostbite is dangerous indeed, but not as deadly as hypothermia. This condition occurs when the temperature of your body grows so cold that it results in death if not addressed. There are many corpses strewn through the Druadach Mountains that have fallen victim to this fate. Let us make sure your body is not among them, walker.

The first step for preventing hypothermia is to remain warm, which Ja'dasha has already covered. Remain dry, seek shelter when needed; this we know. But another risk is drinking alcohol, however pleasurable it may be when traveling in cold climates. The warmth you feel within when your tummy is full of wine is deceitful, for these brews actually trick our bodies into retaining less heat. A healer tried to explain this to Ja'dasha, speaking of increased blood flow and numb limbs. This one understood most of it. She thinks.

Another reason to moderate one's consumption is that rum makes fools of the best of us, and idiots may not know when they are cold. This can be just as true for those who enjoy skooma, greenmote, felldew, and so forth. An impaired mind will do you little good in the coldness of Skyrim. Such recreation should best be saved for warmer climates.

But what are the signs of hypothermia? The first symptom is uncontrollable shivering, like that exhibited by a Khajiit who has a sweet tooth. Then comes the disorientation, confusion, and an apathetic state. Those who begin to suffer hypothermia may even deny feeling cold at all! Trust your eyes more than your ears, walker, when a comrade is in this state. Their body will not lie to you.

Without proper treatment, the symptoms will begin to worsen. Confusion increases, balance is lost, and a great drowsiness is felt. You may even feel the overwhelming urge to fall asleep, regardless of where you stand. Resist the temptation, walker, for you may never awaken from such a slumber. If such drowsiness falls upon a traveling companion, do all you can to keep them awake.

Should the hypothermia continue, you will begin to grow more foolish. Ja'dasha has even seen some Khajiit attempt to strip off their clothing in the middle of a snowstorm. You may begin to grow irritable and stubborn, battling whoever attempts to stop you. Should these symptoms present in a companion, tie them up and carry them to safety if you must. Their life depends on it.

It is when the fighting stops that you must truly worry. You may lose consciousness, or at the very least lose all ability to walk. Your breath will grow weak and your body rigid. Your skin will feel cold and may even turn blue. These are the most severe of signs and could point to imminent death.

No matter the symptoms, a walker with hypothermia must be warmed. Shelter, fire, and blankets are needed. If your clothes are wet, they must be removed and replaced with dry ones. Attempt to share body heat in any way possible once shelter is found. Your companions may stink like a dead horker for all this one cares. The body needs to be warmed in order to begin to heal.

If the hypothermia is severe enough, a healer must be found. It is only through their warming magics that they can increase the internal temperature of the body. A few septims is worth a life, yes?

MEETING A BEAR

Ja'dasha's first trip to Skyrim found her face-to-face with a massive cave bear. This one was frightened, of course, for the bear was very big and had claws that were very large and teeth that were very sharp. But here she is today, writing this guide. How did she do it?

As a note, this advice need not apply to warriors, mages, and the like. If a bear attacks you? Fight it. But for those of us not so physically or magically gifted, there is still much we can do.

Another note: This section does not apply to the far more dangerous creatures found in Skyrim. If you come upon a troll, ice wraith, hagraven, or the like? Then this one cannot help you.

WHAT TO DO

- **Travel in groups.**
  The larger your traveling group is, the more likely a bear is to notice your group and move away before you approach. Do not wander alone.

- **Speak softly.**
  Bears are interested in eating fish and berries, not Khajiit, Nords, or the other races. Speak softly, slowly wave your hands, and stand still. The creature may be curious and approach, but that does not mean it wishes to harm you.

- **Look larger.**
  The larger you seem, the less a bear will be willing to approach. Move to higher ground to make yourself appear larger.

- **Pick up small children.**
  Or small familiars, should you be so inclined. You may have to move very quickly very soon, and you do not want to leave your little ones behind.

- **Stay calm.**
  This is very important, for panicked sounds and movements may lead to an attack. Even if the bear begins to growl or rushes towards you, keep calm unless you are sure the bear means to attack.

continued on next page

- **Escape sideways.**
  When the bear is stationary and calm, move slowly and carefully to the side. Do not allow yourself to trip or fall, as that may startle the bear into an attack.

- **Leave the area.**
  Obvious, no? The bear has claimed that particular piece of forest for that day. Allow them to have it.

WHAT *NOT* TO DO

- **Don't be loud or move quickly.**
  This may spur the bear to attack, and unless you are a skilled warrior or mage, you will not win that fight.

- **Don't run away.**
  Like the dogs we keep as pets, bears like to chase things that run away from them. And you will not be pleased when they catch you. And trust this one, they will catch you. Bears can run as fast as horses.

- **Don't drop your pack.**
  Your pack may be all the protection that remains between you and two very sharp claws.

- **Don't climb trees.**
  Many bears can climb trees, forcing you to choose between facing the beast or a potentially long fall. Save yourself the choice.

- **Don't stand between a cub and mama bear.**
  This is obvious, no? Besides, you would be very upset if a stranger stood between you and your ja'Khajiit.

BEAR ATTACKS

Remember when Ja'dasha said that bears do not wish to attack you? Well, sometimes they do wish to attack you. Life is often tricky in this way. Even trickier is that there are many different species of bears, each of which require different advice for when they attack. We shall concentrate on the most common species for this guide, which are brown and black bears.

BROWN BEAR

The bear has brown fur, yes? Then it is best to play dead. Lay upon your stomach and cover your neck with your hands. Spread your legs to maintain balance so that the bear does not turn you over. Remain in this position until the bear leaves the area.

If the attack persists then you must fight back. Hit the creature's face with whatever you have on hand. The eyes and the nose are particularly sensitive, and striking there may deter the beast. If no items are nearby, then your claws will do. Or fists, for those not so graced.

As a note, there are apparently some bears known as brown bears that are not brown. This is very confusing, but Ja'dasha did not decide such things. Brown bears are always larger than black bears and have a mound of muscles on their upper backs.

BLACK BEAR

If you are facing a black bear, seek a secure location such as a house or carriage. If you must fight, the same advice applies as with a brown bear. Attack the creature's face with sticks, claws, fists, or whatever you have on hand.

CONCLUSION

There are many things to enjoy while visiting Skyrim. Breathtaking views, honeyed mead, and all the salted fish your heart could desire. But atop the mountains, within the caves, and throughout the forests lie dangers of many kinds. Take careful heed of Ja'dasha's advice and you may just survive. And if not? Well, at least you will not be requesting a refund for this book.

This is a joke, of course. Ja'dasha never offers refunds.

HAMMERFELL

Hammerfell is a land of both opportunity and variety. Its coasts are lush and green, home to wealthy port cities and the verdant Banthan Jungle. Head eastward and you will find the harsh Alik'r Desert and the barren stones of Craglorn. To the north are the Dragontail Mountains, their peaks cutting into the sky.

The Redguards hold dominion here. Most choose to live along the flourishing coastline. The many ports along the shore are home to merchants and pirates alike. As you head inward to harsher climes, you will find nomads and farmers. And in every corner of the kingdom can be found proud warriors, for Redguards take pride in their martial prowess. Hammerfell's people are as varied as its land, and from everyone you'll find wisdom and dignity.

Journeying through Hammerfell is never without its dangers. Travel through its lands and you must contend with the heat of the Alik'r Desert. Travel by sea along its coast and you will face storms, swells, and pirates most foul. But you have Ja'dasha's guide, yes? She will tell you how to prepare for such dangers.

SURVIVING THE HEAT

Ja'dasha is no stranger to hot days, coming from the sands of Elsweyr. But the Alik'r Desert is another beast altogether. The heat is more oppressive than this one's mother-in-law, and that is saying something. There is little shade to hide you from the sweltering sun, little water to cool your thirst. And so you must prepare.

As Ja'dasha has noted before, the mages who read this need not worry as much as we mundane folk. Cooling magic, such as wind and rain and ice, are as simple as a snap of the fingers for those magically inclined. But for those not blessed by the art of alteration, we must make due with conventional wisdom.

A PINCH OF PREVENTION

As with all advice this one will give you, a pinch of prevention is better than a barrel of cures. There are many precautions you must take when traveling in extreme heat. How you dress, what you drink, and your planned path can make the difference between life and death.

DRESS IN COOL CLOTHING

Many travelers are overfond of their homeland's fashions: thick wool, expensive furs, even, moons forbid, chain mail. Leave such things in your luggage, walker, and learn from we who walk the sands. Light fabrics in light colors will serve you far better in the heat. The less between you and the blazing sun, the better. However, should you not possess a beautiful coat of fur such as this one, you must watch for sunburn as well. Exposed skin may feel good today, but it will not feel so good come tomorrow.

DRINK WATER (NOT RUM)

This one knows many Khajiit merchants who entered the Alik'r Desert without sufficient water. Well, this one knew such merchants, for they all perished before reaching their destination. The heat will cause sweat to form on your skin, should you not be blessed with luscious fur. This you know. But the more heat, the more sweat, and the less water held within you. And so it must be replenished, but not by rum, nor mead, nor disgusting rotmeth. Water is best to restore what you have lost.

The best way to carry water while traveling through the desert is in a waterskin. It is best to keep a small waterskin on your person at all times, but you can also purchase large ones that can be carried in your caravan or strapped to your horse's

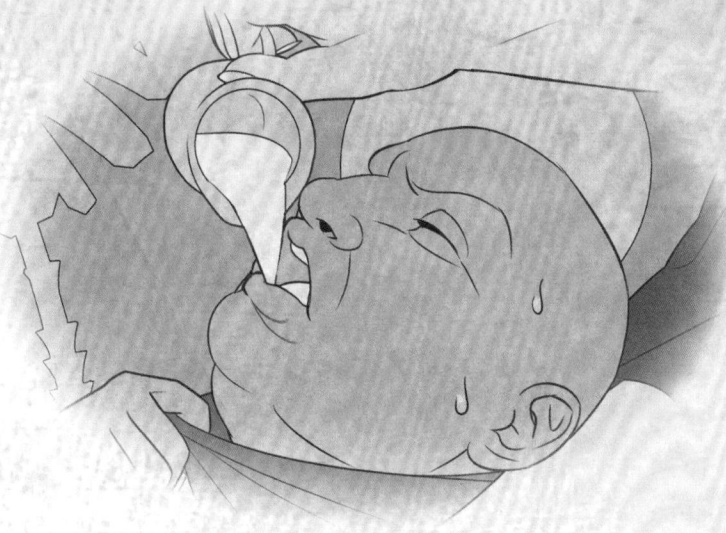

saddle. Barrels will do in a pinch, but they will not retain water nearly as well in the scorching heat.

Most towns and cities will have water for sale, so be sure to stock up when you can. However, do not be shocked when you see the price one must pay for the luxury of water in these desert climates. The Redguards of the Alik'r Desert have spent a lifetime perfecting their means of obtaining water, from oasis springs to rain catcher fields. And they offer these hard-gotten gains at a price to match such dedication.

PLAN FOR SHADE

The desert of Alik'r does not offer much shade, this is true, but there are known places where a desperate walker may find some. Rocky outcroppings, abandoned ruins, sometimes even a small cluster of palm trees will cool your path. Mark such locations on your map, and travel between them. It may make your journey longer, but these short rests may mean the difference between finding your intended destination and finding your ancestors in the next life.

DISEASES OF THE HEAT

Now that we have spoken of preparation, the time has come to speak of cure. What can be done when the heat has claimed you to the point of illness? Restoration magic is Ja'dasha's first suggestion, but if every caravan came with a contingency of mages then there would be no need for this guide (Ja'dasha shudders to think of it). For those of us without magic, there is still much we can do if the heat should strike us.

HEAT CRAMPS

Heat cramps can immobilize even the largest brute. For those who are prone to sweating, the heat can be more torturous. This is especially true if you are traveling by foot, climbing rocky terrain, or performing other strenuous activities. The loss of both moisture and salt due to sweating can result in cramping, muscle pain, and sometimes limb spasms.

Those suffering from heat cramps must relax, eat salty foods, and drink water. The symptoms should go away for most after such a rest. If the cramps persist, it may be a sign of heat exhaustion.

HEAT EXHAUSTION

Those who suffer from heat exhaustion may at first believe themselves to be ill from another disease. Like heat cramps, this illness is due to excessive sweating, which leads to the loss of moisture and salt. It is more likely to strike the elderly and sickly, and the symptoms are many, including:

Weakness	Extreme thirst
Headache	Heavy sweating
Dizziness	Irritability
Nausea	Increased temperature

Those suffering from heat exhaustion need immediate rest, shade, and cool water. Remove as much clothing as you can, especially any footwear. A cool cloth should be applied to the head, face, and neck. Though they may feel nauseous, encourage the afflicted to take frequent sips of water, the cooler, the better.

In the case of heat exhaustion, a healer should be contacted when possible. Head to the closest town or city and pray you have enough septims.

HEATSTROKE

And now we shall speak of the deadliest illness the heat can curse you with. Heatstroke means that the body cannot control its temperature, causing it to rise quickly and drastically. This can lead to permanent harm or even death to those who suffer. It will take more than fervent prayers to S'rendarr to protect you from such a danger, walker. You must always be prepared to handle such an emergency.

If you or a traveling companion is suffering from heatstroke, you must act swiftly. Keep a careful watch for the following symptoms when traveling in the heat:

    Dry, hot skin or heavy sweating
    Confusion, slurred speech, strange emotions
    Unconsciousness
    Seizures
    Extremely increased body temperature

One who suffers from heatstroke must get to a healer as quickly as possible. In the meantime, do all you can to cool down the one inflicted. Take cover in shade, give water, remove as much clothing as possible. Cloths soaked in cool water should be applied to the head, neck, armpits, and groin. If it is possible, soak the clothing of those inflicted with cool water. Do whatever it takes to drop their temperature.

SEA TRAVEL

Sailing along the coast of Iliac Bay may seem a delight, but there are many perils that must be considered for any sea voyage. Ja'dasha, as well traveled as she may be, is no sailor. Do not expect this one to tell you how to tie a knot or hoist the sails. This shall not be a guide to how to sail or maintain a ship, but how to be a well-prepared passenger.

Please note, Ja'dasha will not be discussing the dangers of Sea Elves, Sloads, sea serpents, or other such things, for these threats are best handled by warriors and mages. If you are but a simple traveler, as this one is, and your ship is attacked? Do your best to hide until the fighting is over.

DANGEROUS WEATHER

A storm can be deadly in the best of circumstances, but out in the water this is even more so. Hurricanes, typhoons, and squalls can all lead to sunken ships and drowned crews. What are the dangers and how can you avoid them?

A HEAVY SHIP IS A GOOD SHIP

The waves created by a storm can seem to reach the moons themselves at times. Any ship facing such waves is at risk of being broached, or knocked over onto its side. Broaching leads to sinking, and sinking leads to drowning; this should be easy to understand. But like a drunkard passed out on the sands, a heavy belly can prevent such rolling.

Filling the bottom of your ship with cargo will help prevent a ship from being broached. If you are not supplying such cargo, be sure to speak with the captain about such things. An empty ship presents a risk you must carefully weigh.

REMAIN ABOARD AND HOLD ON

As a passenger, you will generally have the luxury of remaining within the hold of the ship during storms. In emergencies, however, you can be asked to help on deck. Under the cutting rain and against surging waves, you may feel that your life would be safer out on the open sea. This is a foolish, desperate thought. A sailor overboard is a sailor dead, especially amidst the chaos of a storm. Some even tie themselves to the deck with ropes, though this is very dangerous if the ship begins to sink.

Whatever happens, remain on the deck. Your life depends on it, walker.

KEEP SAILING

Ja'dasha has known some to weep and cry at the sight of a storm, begging the captain to turn back or to lay anchor. And a good captain will ignore such pleas and sail ahead, for there is no way to outrun a storm and no good in waiting it out.

The best course of action is to sail into the waves in order to break through them, as the bow of the ship is far stronger than the stern. This will avoid damaging the ship or taking on too much water. This also keeps the rudder in the sea, which is necessary for the ship to steer. Without control, the ship would be at the mercy of the winds and rain.

AVOID LAND

Land may seem safe when caught in a storm, but it presents its own dangers. The heavy winds can easily cause a ship to strike the shore, tearing its bottom. Even if close to land, a sinking ship is likely to lead to a drowned crew, especially in the middle of a storm.

SHIP SICKNESS

Close quarters means that sickness spreads quickly among a crew. It is best to travel with a healer if the captain does not already employ one. Without a healer, however, the best you can do is be vigilant of any sign of disease.

SEASICKNESS

Those who have never ridden on a boat may find themselves nauseated by the experience. This sickness is caused by the motion of the boat bobbing up and down on the waves. While not (usually) deadly, this can make even the shortest voyage an uncomfortable one. Here are some common symptoms to keep watch for:

Fatigue	Vomiting
Irritability	Headaches
Cold sweat	Pale skin
Nausea	Rapid breathing

Ja'dasha's cousin was cursed by this illness, making his life as a sailor a rather short one. His seasickness came upon him very suddenly on the first day after leaving harbor. Unfortunately the ship was unable to turn back by the time he began to vomit. And then he did not stop vomiting for the entire three weeks of his voyage, praying to Khenarthi to make the voyage swifter each day. Now he cleans stables for a living.

If this one's cousin had read her guide, however, there are many things he could have done to ease his seasickness:

Eat well. Drink plenty of water and avoid greasy foods that may upset the stomach. Avoid alcohol and smoking (this one knows that is easier said than done, but your stomach will thank you).

Stay above deck. Try to stay on the deck during the day if possible. The fresh air will do you a world of good.

Gaze into the distance. Look upon the horizon and keep your gaze there. This one has no idea why this works to calm seasickness, but trust her, it does.

Rest. Lie on your back and close your eyes when not on deck. Try to get some sleep while you're at it. It will certainly make for a faster voyage, if nothing else.

Even if you are wise enough to heed Ja'dasha's words, not all can tolerate such sickness. So it is wise to make sure your first voyage is a short one. No need to be trapped for weeks on end, like this one's dull-clawed cousin.

SCURVY

Unlike some other illnesses, scurvy cannot be caught or passed on. Rather, it is an effect of the absence of a healthy diet, specifically fruits and vegetables. On long journeys out on the sea, this disease is all too common, as provisions must be long lasting and easy to store. This generally leads to an absence of the food needed to stave off this ailment.

The symptoms of scurvy generally start with weakness, lethargy, irritability, and sadness. Your joints and legs will become painful, and your gums will bleed and swell. Your skin will develop red or blue spotting, especially along the shins. Bruises develop easily. In the end, this disease can and will lead to death. The only cure is a proper diet. Be sure that either yourself or the ship's crew has prepared proper provisions for the journey.

WALKER OVERBOARD

Sea voyages would not be so deadly if the ship were not surrounded by, well, the sea. You may be swept overboard by storm winds, or pushed overboard by a jealous nephew. Whatever the reason, it is best to be prepared in case you find yourself unexpectedly in the water.

HOW TO NOT DROWN

Learn to swim. Simple, no? There will be no drowning if you are able to swim back to the ship. A good precaution to take before boarding a vessel.

Do not drink (excessively). This one has been on many long voyages. She understands that there is little to do sometimes but drink. But do not drink so much that you may stumble overboard.

Stay near a friend (with rope). Having a companion with you increases the likelihood that someone will notice you have fallen overboard. Have them throw you a ladder or rope to help you climb back onto the deck.

Stay calm. The flailing and the screaming will do nothing but make you drown faster. Try to remain calm and act rationally.

Float. If you do not know how to swim, there is still a good chance you will be able to float. Flip onto your back and keep your mouth above water. This will be far easier if you stay calm.

Call for help. No friend nearby? There should be someone on the deck at all times, and that someone can provide aid. Just pray they hear you.

SHARKS IN THE WATER

There are many, many, many horrible things in the sea. Sea serpents, krakens, and Sloads, to name only a few. If you encounter such horrors? Not even all of Ja'dasha's wisdom can save you, walker. But should you encounter a shark? Well, sharks we can deal with.

Stay calm. This one understands that this is easier said than done, but it must be done. Sharks are attracted to movement, especially splashing. It may provoke them to attack.

Keep eye contact. Sharks tend to attack their prey from behind, so make sure that there is no such opening. Keeping an eye on the creature will make them hesitate.

Slowly back away. Preferably toward the ship you have fallen from.

Attack eyes and gills. If the shark does attack you, these are the best areas to aim for. With luck you will drive the beast off.

ADRIFT AT SEA

So your ship has sunk and you were lucky enough to climb aboard the dinghy. If you were clever, you will have brought fresh water and food along with you. If you were in a hurry, well, Ja'dasha cannot judge. But she can give you some advice on how to survive your ordeal.

Keep cool. As spoken of in earlier sections, the sun is now your enemy and keeping cool is paramount to survival. Stay under any shade you can create and try to keep hydrated as much as possible. If you or your companions suffer from heat exhaustion or heatstroke, try to cool them down.

Keep hydrated. Thirst will kill you faster than hunger will, and this is the most likely reason you will die. However, you will die a lot faster if you drink sea water. The salt will only increase your thirst, leading to an earlier death.

Keep hope. Such an ordeal is sure to test your sanity. If you have escaped with others, talking will generally help pass the time and keep your mind off the situation at hand. Speak of your hopes for the future, and what you will do when you are rescued.

Remember that not all hope is lost. Even a dinghy adrift at sea will be kept moving by the waves, traveling an extraordinary distance each day. There is still a chance another boat will find you, or you will come upon land.

WOUND CARE

While the Redguards are well regarded for their warriors, they should be just as highly praised for their healers. Their wisdom is not only limited to the magical school of restoration, but also includes the more mundane ways in which any of us may tend to our wounds. And while having a mage around to heal all that ails us is the best circumstance a traveler may hope for, not all of us will be so lucky. And so Ja'dasha passes on to you the wisdom she learned during time spent in Hammerfell about such matters.

As a precaution, all serious wounds should be seen by a healer. This is especially true if a wound has grown infected or is causing a great deal of pain. Restoration magic may not come cheap, but it does certainly save lives.

CLEANING WOUNDS

A small wound can grow into a large problem if not properly cared for. The first step to preventing infection is to properly clean and bandage your wound.

Wash your hands. Your wound is already dirty, no? Then it is best not to have it grow dirtier from your filthy fingers. Wash your hands thoroughly.

Apply pressure. If the wound is still bleeding, pressure will help stop the flow of blood. Use a clean cloth to do so.

Cleanse the wound. Once the bleeding has stopped, it is time to wash the wound with water and soap. Use tweezers (or clean fingers) to pluck out any large objects. Pat the wound dry once it is completely clean.

Apply healing salve. If in your possession, apply a healing salve to the wound. Follow any healer instructions you may possess.

Bandage the wound. Allow the wound to dry completely before applying bandages. There is some skill in doing this, which this one will cover in the next section.

Repeat. Wounds do not magically heal overnight, and they also do not magically stay clean. Unless, of course, you are using magic. For the rest of us, we will need to repeat these steps until the wound has healed.

HOW TO SPOT INFECTION

Even the cleanest wounds can become infected. This can be healed with regular cleanings and healing salves, but a healer should be consulted if a wound is infected for more than one or two days. Keep careful watch for the symptoms of an infected wound:

- Nausea and vomiting
- Aches, pains, fever, and chills
- An unpleasant odor emanating from the wound
- Yellow or green discharge
- Warm skin or red streaks around the wound

BANDAGING WOUNDS

A clean wound will not stay clean for very long if there is not a proper bandage to protect it. Bandages should be replaced once a day, or after becoming damp or sullied. Be sure that the bandages themselves are also clean of any impurities.

Before applying a bandage, clean the wound. Ja'dasha has explained these steps in the section above. Read this first.

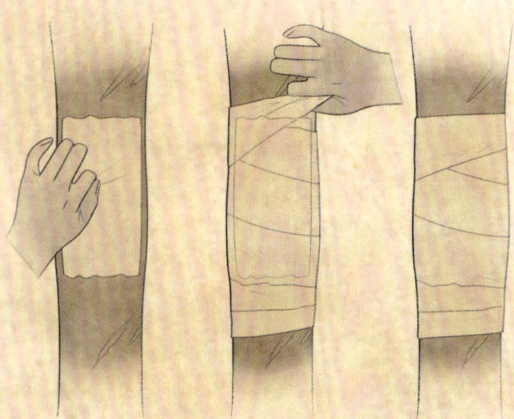

Apply a dressing pad. This is a thick pad of gauze laid directly on top of the wound. It will staunch the blood and protect the wound. Be sure the dressing pad is larger than the wound it is covering.

Wrap the bandage. Place the unrolled bandage across the dressing pad, placed with a longer and shorter length on either side of the pad. First wrap the shorter length of the bandage around the injured area, leaving enough of the end of the length hanging free to allow you to tie it. Next wrap the longer length around the injured part completely to secure the dressing pad.

Tie the bandage. Tie the longer and shorter lengths of the bandage together directly on top of the dressing pad to apply pressure to the wound. This will help stop further bleeding.

Check circulation. Press a claw (or nail) hard against the skin near the wound for a few seconds. The color of the skin should lighten noticeably. If the color does not return to the flesh in a few moments, the bandage is too tight and you need to loosen it.

Reapply. Bandages must be changed once a day, when sullied, or if blood begins to drench the gauze. This is key to preventing infection.

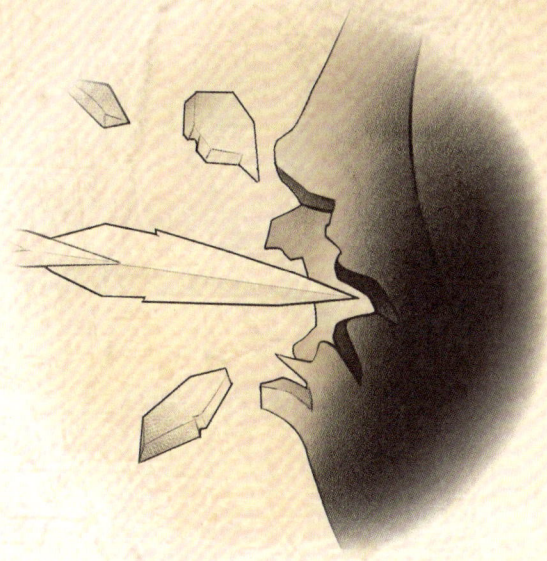

REMOVING ARROWS

Should you find yourself on the wrong end of an archer's art, it is always best for a skilled healer to remove the arrow. The bleeding that occurs after removal is dangerous, and must be properly tended to. But if there is no such healer available? Then you must do your best.

Arrowheads generally come in two forms: a narrow, spiked shape, typically used for piercing armor; and the perhaps more familiar broad-headed, triangular shape with a pointed tip and a wide base. Depending on which arrow you are attacked with, the best method for removing them differs drastically.

ARMOR-PIERCING ARROW

An arrow of this type has a narrow, spike or dagger-like arrowhead that enables it to pierce an opponent's armor. These arrows can be directly removed from the body. Note, however, that removing the arrow will cause the wound to begin bleeding heavily. Be sure that you are prepared to apply pressure and stop the bleeding after the arrow is extracted. Follow, of course, with cleaning and bandaging of the wound to prevent infection.

If the arrow has hit a vulnerable part of your body, such as your chest, stomach, or neck, then it is best to leave the arrow be until a proper healer is found. If these areas are damaged they may lead to a walker bleeding out, perhaps fatally.

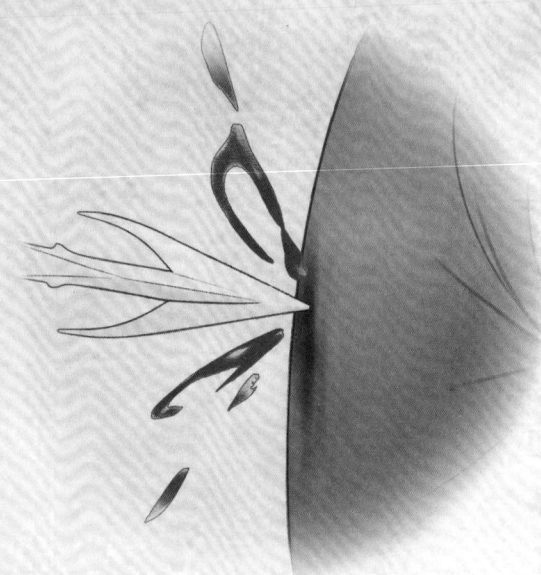

BROAD-HEADED ARROW

This arrow is a different beast altogether. Due to the triangular shape of the arrowhead, it cannot be safely removed without its wide base pulling on the injury and causing further damage. Ideally a surgeon would remove this type of arrow for you. This is especially true if it has lodged in a vulnerable part of your body, namely your chest, stomach, or neck.

If this type of arrow has penetrated a limb and a healer cannot be found, you can push the arrow through until it has completely penetrated your flesh on the other side of the limb. You can then cut off the arrowhead and remove the shaft. This is incredibly painful, and once again is best done under the supervision of one with healing experience.

BROKEN BONES

One day Ja'dasha and her niece were traveling through the rocky crags of the Forgotten Wastes. This one took her eyes off the little ja'Khajiit for but one moment before she heard a loud cry. She looked behind her to find her niece clutching her arm, howling in pain. Luckily, Ja'dasha had the wisdom to know just what to do.

Breaking a bone while traveling is more likely than you may suspect, especially when the land is uneven. This is especially true for the young, the old, and the feeble. While a healer should be consulted, there is much you can do for those inflicted with the injury.

Examine the injury. If the limb is bruised, swollen, and discolored, then this is a simple fracture, which is good! If the bone has pierced the flesh or has created a deformity beneath the flesh, this is a compound fracture, which is bad.

Set the bone (if you know how). A bone out of place will need to be set back into place. This is best done only if you have training as a healer, as doing this incorrectly may result in more harm than good. For a compound fracture, you may even increase the bleeding and kill the patient. Not a good way to end a journey, walker.

Splint or tourniquet? A splint will always be needed for a simple fracture. A compound fracture that is heavily bleeding will need a tourniquet. Simple.

How to make a splint. If there are any wounds that are lightly bleeding, be sure to clean and bandage them first. Place long, solid objects (such as branches) on either side of the limb. They should not touch any wounds if possible. Wrap the objects with a rope, cord, or cloth. Do not do this so tightly that blood circulation in the limb is inhibited.

How to make a tourniquet. This is only needed if the wound is heavily bleeding. Find a wide piece of rope, cord, or cloth to wrap a finger's length above the wound. Tie it tightly to slow the flow of blood. Head to a healer quickly afterward.

CONCLUSION

From sweeping deserts to jungle depths, from harbor ports to craggy ruins, the land of Hammerfell is one filled with beauty and mystery. And danger, of course, which is why you have bought this guide. Keep your wits about you and your supplies on hand, and you may just make it out of this land with your arms and legs intact.

Unless you manage to insult a swordmaster. That is a predicament not even the wise Ja'dasha can advise you out of.

ELSWEYR

So you have decided to walk the sands of Elsweyr, walker? Ja'dasha cannot blame you. From the sun-drenched savannas of Reaper's March to the moons-drenched waters of Topal Bay, there is no land more beautiful than the home of the Khajiit. Whether you seek awe-inspiring temples, tropical paradises, or a bottle of sweet cane mead, there is no greater place than Ja'dasha's homeland.

To the north lies Anequina, known for its harsh badlands and dry plains. The Khajiit here are hardened warriors who have done much to survive. To the south you shall find Pellitine, home of jungles, river basins, and lush farmland. Those blessed enough to live in these lands (this one included) know far more luxury and greenery than our northern kin. This great wealth brings with it many hardships, however, as we must contend with bandits, pirates, and thieves of every stripe.

To travel through Elsweyr, you must learn to be wary of its dark underbelly. Ja'dasha will cover a great many topics regarding the seedier side of her great homeland. From kidnappings to thieves, and everything in between, this one will be your guide.

BE WARY OF THIEVES

Traveling through the cities of Elsweyr can be an exciting experience for many. From the gorgeous sights of our beautiful buildings to the delicious sweetbreads baked to perfection, there is no place quite like them. But just as a wondrous antique or beautiful outfit catches your eye, you go to pull out your coin purse to find … nothing. For you have been a victim of one of the many thieves that roam the streets.

There are many thieves in Tamriel, from country bandits to city rogues, but none quite so skilled as the Khajiit. After all, it is no small coincidence that the Thieves Guild has made its home in Abah's Landing, or so the rumor goes. To enter Elsweyr is to put every septim you own on the line, and there have been many who have left this one's homeland without a coin to their name. How can you prevent such a thing? By reading the wise words of Ja'dasha, of course.

HIDDEN SEPTIMS

Pickpockets are only so adept at filching septims. Should you hide your coins away in an inner pocket or otherwise unusual location, you are far less likely to fall victim. Ja'dasha has known some Khajiit who have hidden coins in their belts, hats, boots, and even brassieres—anywhere that a thief would have trouble putting their paws into.

However, this hidden location will not be so hidden if you are constantly pulling coins out. This is why it is best to keep a small amount of septims in an easy-to-retrieve location, such as a pocket or coin purse. When thieves see you pay for wares, they will not know the secret location that houses the bulk of your fortune.

FALSE FORTUNE

Keeping all of your prized possessions on you at all times is not possible for many travelers. As such, you may need to keep some items in your lodgings. How can you be sure that your belongings will not be taken by thieves when you are away?

One way is to leave a small coin purse beneath your pillow. Thieves are usually opportunistic and wary of being caught. If they quickly find a coin purse, despite how small a fortune that coin purse may contain, they may choose to leave before searching the rest of the room. A small price to pay for the safety of your other possessions.

Ja'dasha must also recommend placing your possessions in a bank if you truly wish for safety. While the Khajiit may be renowned thieves, our banks are just as renowned for their safety. This may have something to do with the fact that most bankers are former thieves themselves. But this one digresses.

ALWAYS BE WARY

Even with hidden septims and false fortunes, there are many situations that are best avoided. Walking the city streets at night or visiting certain establishments may lend itself to danger more often than not. A Khajiit that has you held at knifepoint will not be afraid to strip you naked to make sure they take every last septim. It is best to ask a local Khajiit which areas of the city are safe.

Always keep an eye out for suspicious activity. If someone seems to be following you, try to enter a busy location or find a nearby city guard. Travel with your companions and try not to be separated. And, by the moons, do not brag about your fortune or flash your coins about. There is no need to place a target on your back.

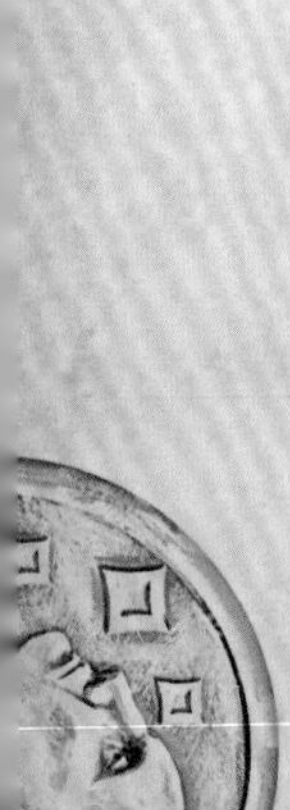

SURVIVING AN ABDUCTION

Your fortune is not the only thing in need of protection, walker. Be careful of those who mean to abduct you. Perhaps the Red Hands or Ruddy Fangs mean to make some coin by selling you to Dark Elves. Or perhaps Euraxia Tharn decided you know something she wishes to learn, and sent her soldiers after you. Or perhaps the New Moon Cult means to add you to their dark ranks. Always know that your body can be as easily stolen as your coin purse.

Whether you are captured for ransom, information, or to be entered into forced labor, there are many things you can do to increase your chances of surviving such a situation, starting with not being abducted at all.

ESCAPING

When you have been abducted, it is best to first try to escape. Run away from your abductors while calling loudly for help. Aim to enter a crowded location where you can seek aid. If you are caught by one of your abductors, fight back.

For those of you who are not warriors or mages, self-defense can be a daunting prospect. Try to fight back any way you can, even if this involves biting and scratching. Aim for your abductor's groin, eyes, nose, and throat. If there are nearby objects you can employ as weapons, use them! Small objects can be used to throw at or strike your attacker, while larger ones might be deployed as a barrier so your attacker cannot grab you. Do all you can to force them to let you go so you can continue your escape.

However, if you are captured, there is now only one choice left before you.

DO NOT STRUGGLE ONCE CAPTURED

Your abductors have already chosen to capture you for nefarious purposes. They will not flinch at the thought of beating, bludgeoning, or otherwise harming you. So it is best to comply with their demands and not struggle at this point. Remain polite and compliant. Do not move around, squirm, or attempt to escape. It is best to keep yourself as healthy as possible. Any violence against you may harm your chances of escaping later.

If they seek to drug you, it is best to comply with this as well. Your opponents most likely seek to make you unconscious and silently move you to a new location.

Should you fight against this plan, it is likely they will beat you unconscious. Ja'dasha does not need to tell you that one fate is far worse than the other. Comply and take the drugs.

If you are conscious when transported, take note of your travels. If you are blindfolded, it is still possible to listen to your surroundings. Try to keep track of how far you travel and in which general direction. Any information you can gain may help you if there is a chance to escape.

FOCUS ON SURVIVAL

Once the abductors have reached their destination, it is time to focus on surviving. Escape should only be attempted after careful planning, and only if you believe your captors do not plan to let you leave.

1. BE OBSERVANT

Take note of every detail you can of your surroundings. Where are you being held? What do your abductors want? What activities do they perform? Is there a rank among them? The more information you can obtain, the better your chances of survival. And, should you escape, the better chance you have of finding help and reporting your abductors to the proper authorities.

2. BE OBEDIENT

Any attempt to fight back or otherwise rebel against your captors will only lead to beatings, neglect, and possibly even torture. It is best to remain calm and polite at all times, always following the instructions you are given. The less you are harmed and the better you are treated, the more strength you will have to survive and possibly escape.

3. BE COMMUNICATIVE

In a practical sense, it is best to answer any questions that you are asked as truthfully as possible to avoid angering your captors. However, it is also best to try to emotionally connect with your abductors. Speak to them of your family and interests. Remind them that you are a person, not a mere victim. This may earn you sympathy in return.

It must be noted that you should not pretend to have sympathy with your abductors. Avoid topics that may anger them, such as religion or politics. Be sincere in all you say or do, lest they believe you are tricking them.

Politely ask for items that you need, such as blankets, food, and water. Keep your requests reasonable and easy to provide. Again, this must be paired with complacency and politeness on your part, and perhaps a fair bit of sympathy from your abductors. The less you seem like a threat, the less harsh you shall be treated.

4. BE PATIENT

An unsuccessful escape can lead to beatings, torture, or possibly death. Thus it is best to be patient when abducted. If you believe there is a chance you will be rescued, wait for help to arrive. If you are positive that escape is your only option, wait for the best opportunity possible. Either way, you may be held for quite a while.

Mental and physical exercises will help keep you alert and healthy. Meditation and prayer can help keep you calm and stable. Whatever you choose to do, be sure to do it quietly and without drawing attention to yourself.

ESCAPE (IF POSSIBLE)

As stated before, escape is a dangerous undertaking that must be used as a last resort. You may notice that your abductors have stopped feeding you and have begun acting nervously, signaling that they plan to kill you. Or you may learn that they intend to sell you into forced labor. Whatever the situation, escape must be something you are willing to risk your life for.

1. PLAN WITH OTHER CAPTIVES

If you are fortunate enough to be held with other captives, it is best to try to plan any escape attempts with them to increase your chances. This must be done as secretly as possible to not alert your captors. At the very least, it is best to come up with a code word for when an escape attempt will be made.

2. ACT CAUTIOUSLY

Put all your careful observations to good use. Plan the best time for escape, such as when your abductors are gone or asleep. Observe the best escape route possible. Plan your actions with your fellow captives if possible.

2. HEAD TO A SAFE LOCATION

If you are able to escape, it is best to find the nearest town, city, or group who can help. Speak to those in authority and give as much detail that you can about the encounter. Seek a healer's attention as soon as you can. Be sure you are in a safe location where your abductors cannot find you.

BE RESCUED (EVEN BETTER)

Even if you have the good fortune of being rescued, there are still precautions to take. There may be a situation in which those who've come to rescue you believe that you are dangerous. Ensure this does not happen by dropping to the floor with your hands resting on your head, showing that you are not a threat. State that you are a hostage and comply with all their orders.

HOW TO SURVIVE A PLUNGE FROM A WATERFALL

You may be confused that Ja'dasha would see fit to give you such advice. But when there is a ferocious senche-cat bearing down on you and a sheer cliff to your back? Then a nearby waterfall may not seem all that unwelcoming. Trust this one on such matters.

Hold your breath. This should be done just before you have reached the edge.

Position your legs first. Point your feet toward the edge of the waterfall so that you fall feet first. Cross them tightly so they do not splay as you hit the water.

Tuck your chin, wrap your arms. Tuck your chin into your chest and tightly wrap one arm over your mouth and the other above your head. This is to keep your neck from breaking.

Tense your body. All of your muscles should be tensed as tightly as possible. And remember! Tuck your chin into your chest! Wrap your arms around your head! And cross those legs!

Close your eyes and mouth. This is to avoid ingesting water and damaging your sight when you hit the water.

Swim away. You must leave the bottom of the falls before surfacing, for the falling water can be very powerful. Surface too soon and you may be pushed back under the water.

A GUIDE TO FURSTOCKS

There are many who come to Elsweyr without realizing just how many forms the moons have blessed we Khajiit with. And so they make many mistakes, such as trying to hunt down this one's grandmother. That was certainly a fun wedding.

For those not familiar, there are seventeen distinct forms that we Khajiit can take, commonly called furstocks. Our forms depend on which phase of the two moons we are born under. We hold such things quite sacred, for it is by the moons' will that we are given our beautiful forms, not the will of we mere Khajiit.

Ja'dasha will kindly explain every furstock you may meet in Elsweyr, and she promises to not trick you. This will not be so with her kin, for making fools of tourists is a great pleasure among the Khajiit.

✦ ALFIQ AND ALFIQ-RAHT

The Alfiq and Alfiq-raht are very confusing to travelers. Many who visit Elsweyr believe them to be mere housecats, due to their diminutive size and quadrupedal nature. (Quadrupedal is a fancy term for walking on four legs, as many Khajiit do, instead of two. Or so this one overheard while visiting a mages hall in Rimmen.) This is a foolish thing to do, for the Alfiq deserve much respect. After all, they are among the most powerful mages and wisest scholars the Khajiit have to offer.

The Alfiq rarely travel outside of their homeland due to the ignorance of outsiders, though many are kidnapped by tourists who are ignorant of our forms. You shall note the Alfiq by their clothing, which most choose to wear. If you are unsure if you are in the presence of an Alfiq or a housecat, you may kindly greet them and see if they respond. This is common sense that many visitors do not seem to possess.

The Alfiq-raht are very similar to their Alfiq kin, only being slightly larger. It is best not to presume if a Khajiit is Alfiq or Alfiq-raht, and instead allow them to inform you. (Alfiq-raht are especially sensitive to this, as they are quite proud of their larger size.)

❋ CATHAY AND CATHAY-RAHT

Ja'dasha knows a great deal about the Cathay, for she is one. We are most noted for our stature, as we are the height of many of the other races of Tamriel. Our bodies are covered in beautiful fur, which can present in a variety of colors and patterns. Our fangs are long and large, and we are blessed with sharp claws on both our hands and feet.

Our cousins the Cathay-raht are slightly larger than we, and have been known to make exceptional warriors. The Imperials once named them jaguar-men, which is a silly name indeed. Many do not look like jaguars, and many are not men.

❋ TOJAY AND TOJAY-RAHT

The Tojay and Tojay-raht are much like we Cathay. They live within the southern ma rshes and jungles of Elsweyr. There is more to say, but Ja'dasha will not be the one to say it.

❋ SUTHAY AND SUTHAY-RAHT

The Suthay are also much like the Cathay and Tojay, only their legs are more bestial. A High Elf scholar once told Ja'dasha that the fancy term for creatures like the Suthay who walk upon the sands with their toes is digitigrade. This is one of the reasons they make exceptional sneaks and thieves.

The Suthay-raht, as you may have guessed, is a slightly larger furstock. Ja'dasha knows of few other differences, though the Suthay-raht tend to have a harder time fitting into small spaces.

❋ DAGI AND DAGI-RAHT

The Dagi and Dagi-raht are the second smallest furstock of the Khajiit, larger only than the Alfiq. Other than their diminutive statue, they look much like the Cathay. Many live in Tenmar Forest, for they are skilled climbers who love to make their homes in the trees. There are said to be entire communities of Dagi living in the branches, though Ja'dasha has never visited one herself. They also share the Alfiq's skill with magic.

The Dagi-raht are slightly larger than their Dagi cousins, and are quite proud of that fact. Unfortunately, this difference may be the slightest among all the furstocks, and even we Khajiit may have trouble noticing the difference. This is never very well received by a Dagi-raht, so it is best not to make assumptions.

⚙ OHMES AND OHMES-RAHT

Many mistake the Ohmes and Ohmes-raht as Bosmer, or Wood Elf, for they are the only Khajiit to not have received the blessing of fur. They do, however, possess a tail, showing that the moons have a kindness for even the most pitiful. They will often paint or even tattoo their faces with feline markings to avoid being mistaken for a Wood Elf, which is certainly understandable.

As with all other furstocks, the Ohmes-raht are slightly larger in stature than the Ohmes.

⚙ PAHMAR AND PAHMAR-RAHT

The Pahmar are larger than even the Suthay-raht, and are often employed as bodyguards and warriors. A Pahmar-raht, as you may imagine, is even larger. Most resemble senche-tigers, and are twice as deadly when provoked.

⚙ SENCHE AND SENCHE-RAHT

Like their Alfiq cousins, many ignorant outsiders will often believe a Senche to be a creature rather than a Khajiit. However, a Senche is a great deal larger than an Alfiq. The Senche-raht, the larger of the two, has the honor of being the largest furstock. They are similar in appearance to senche-cats, walking upon all four of their paws. Their forelimbs are thick and their hind limbsare one and a half times long.

During battle, Senches and Senche-rahts will sometimes allow other Khajiit to ride upon their backs. However, it is a grave insult to compare a Senche to a mere mount or beast of burden. They are quite capable of speaking, reading, and performing magic, just as any other Khajiit. An outsider speaks down to the Senche at their own risk, for there is little patience to be found within their mighty hearts.

 THE MANE

Revered and honored throughout Elsweyr, there can only be one Mane alive at any given time. They are born during the dark moon, when both Jode and Jone are gone from the sky. Their name comes from the tradition of the Khajiit shaving their manes in a show of respect, and of the Mane braiding these furs into their own locks. Given how impractical this became, the Mane eventually wore a headdress that displayed locks of the Mane's tribe and its warrior guard.

If you have the honor to meet with the Mane, treat them with the dignity of any king, queen, or emperor. For they are destined to lead the Khajiit by the power of the blessed moons.

CONCLUSION

The beauty of Elsweyr cannot merely be described, but must be seen in all its glory. Whether you seek the coastal cities with all their history and culture, or the green grasses of moon-sugar cane in the water basins, there is no end of delights to be experienced. Truly there is no greater destination to visit in Tamriel, wherever you hail from. In practical considerations, of course, Elsweyr is also a great hub of trade and commerce. If you are a merchant of any note, it is likely you will travel there eventually.

Many travelers enter Ja'dasha's homeland unaware of both its wonders and many dangers. But not you, walker, for you had the wisdom to purchase and read this great work of wisdom. And so you are prepared to walk the sands with the Khajiit.

BLACK MARSH

So you wish to venture into Black Marsh, yes? A foolish endeavor for all but the scale-covered Argonians. The land is cruel and inhospitable compared to even the harshest regions of Tamriel. The marshes are filled with poisonous plants, venomous creatures, and flesh-eating insects. There may be some who can find beauty in the twisted branches of the trees that grow upon the land, of the overgrown greenery and stinking swamps … but not Ja'dasha.

Many Argonians are inhospitable to outsiders, and for good reason. The Imperials tried to build cities and roads and trade, but they quickly decayed, just as everything does in those swamps. There are many who see Black Marsh only as an ample source of slaves, and little else. The Dark Elves are constant invaders in these lands, capturing Argonians to labor in their farms (a fate shared by us Kahjiit, this one must note).

Should you find Argonians who are willing to speak to you, you will note them to be quite outlandish. They are connected to nature like few other races in Tamriel, and often speak in riddles. Their customs are strange and their religion even stranger. But still, they are honest folk. Should you decipher their riddles, you are likely to find truth in their words.

If you are absolutely set on traveling through Black Marsh, then you have made a very good choice in buying Ja'dasha's book. For even the most prepared and well read of travelers will struggle to survive in the swamps of Argonia.

DANGERS OF THE MARSH

A marsh is a low-lying area that is prone to flooding in the wet seasons. It remains waterlogged most of the year, which means you will encounter a great deal of mud and muck. Do not expect your boots to make it back unscathed if you travel through these lands, for roads are few and far between.

Traveling through the marsh is not just a danger to your footwear, however. Ja'dasha will warn of the most notable hazards, but it is truly best to travel with a guide if possible. There are none who know the swamps of this land better than the Argonians raised in them.

BE CAREFUL WHERE YOU STEP

It is not enough that you must walk through muck while you traverse Black Marsh, but you must also be careful of what you tread upon! For a misstep may leave you with a twisted ankle, waterlogged belongings, and worse.

THE RIGHT EQUIPMENT

While many Argonians run around their homeland without shoes, we outsiders cannot afford to be so lax in our use of footwear. It is best to obtain sturdy boots that completely cover your feet and ankles. The bottoms of these shoes must have good traction, which means that you must clean your boots periodically as the bottoms become clogged with mud.

Another item of great help is a sturdy walking stick, or even better, sturdy walking poles. These sharp-tipped instruments help you as you tread along the slippery muck. Always remember to keep one pole firmly planted within the earth to maintain your balance as you stride forward.

POSTURE AND TECHNIQUE

Maintaining a tight belly will help center your body and achieve greater balance. (A great tip for those who wish to try tightrope walking as well, or so Ja'dasha has been told.) This will be especially useful as you stride downhill.

Relaxing your neck and shoulders will also help you keep balanced. Not an easy feat when one is constantly sliding on muck and mire! The anxiety brought on by having to be ever vigilant about slipping or falling cause many to lift their shoulders and tighten their neck. Keep careful watch of such reactions, for they shall only hinder you. Maintain a large gap between your shoulders and ears.

A strong arm swing can also help with walking through mud, though it is best to avoid extending your elbows beyond the back of your hips. This is especially important if you are using poles or walking sticks, for you always want these items to be planted in front of you.

WALKING THE WALK

How to walk within the swamps of Black Marsh is such an important topic that Ja'dasha has given it its own section.

As any of sound mind, you will wish to travel through the swamps as quickly as possible. However, a fast stride can lead to much slipping. Shorten your stride and slow your steps to help keep balance. You will thank Ja'dasha later, for traveling with a twisted ankle will slow you down far more than taking cautious steps!

Where you step is just as important as how you step. A guide will be essential for this, for they will lead you along the safest paths. Even those paths, however, will be filled with holes, slippery puddles, and tangling roots. Watch where you step, and take careful note of the ground ahead of you.

QUICKSAND

Ja'dasha once thought that quicksand was a scary story told to keep ja'Khajiit from wandering too far, but it does indeed exist within the ruinous swamps of Black Marsh. If you find yourself sinking quickly into the mud, do not panic. Walk slowly back in the direction you came from until you find the edge of solid ground. Remain calm, for thrashing will only make you sink faster.

POWER OF POISONS

If there is one thing you must learn from Ja'dasha's amazing book, it is that everything in Black Marsh is trying to kill you. Even the most edible plants will not sit well within an outsider's tummy. Trust this one. Every plant is coated or filled with venoms, poisons, or other nasty things. A tiny bite can be enough to kill.

So let us try to avoid this, yes?

FOUL FORAGING

Ja'dasha is sad to inform you that, yes, there are travelers who try to eat the plants in Black Marsh without a proper guide. You, of course, would never be so foolish. But should you have little ones (or idiots) traveling with you, it is best to know what to do should someone ingest a poisonous plant.

First, you should consult a healer if at all possible. Describe the type of plant eaten and how much of it was eaten. An Argonian healer would obviously be best in such cases, for they will have knowledge of which plants are poisonous and what remedies are needed. Any healer will do in a pinch, of course, especially those trained in restoration magic.

If no healer is available, have the one who is ill drink many glasses of water. The hope is to force them to vomit, purging their stomach of the poisons. Another method is to stick a finger down their throat or have them drink vomit-inducing medicines, which someone may have on hand. Allow the victim to vomit several times, and have them checked by a healer as soon as you can.

While there may be plants that are perfectly safe for most to eat, your stomach may be less forgiving. Should you be sensitive to many foods, it is best to forgo the joys of foraging. An upset stomach, hives, or rashes will do you little good as you travel through the wilderness of Black Marsh.

VENOMOUS BITES

Even if you do not wish to take a bite out of the swamp, it may choose to take a bite out of you. All manner of venomous wildlife lurks upon and beneath the many roots on your travels. What do you do if you happen to be bitten by such?

PREVENTION

As Ja'dasha has said before, watch where you walk when traveling through swamps. If you see a creature in the road ahead of you, try your best to avoid it. This is especially true for creatures that you know to be poisonous, such as many snakes.

A walking stick will also help with more than just your balance. If a walking stick strikes the ground ahead of your feet, creatures are much more likely to attack the stick rather than your leg. It is also a good practice to wear tall boots, thick socks, and long pants. The more you can protect your feet and legs, the better off you will be.

Last, it is best to travel during the day, or with torches lighting your way if you must move at night. Darkness can lead you to step upon creatures that are best not stepped upon.

SYMPTOMS

Within Black Marsh, it is always best to be cautious after being bitten by a creature. There are many telltale signs that a bite is venomous, however.

The amount of venom will vary from creature to creature, but the symptoms are very clear. Venomous bites are very painful and quickly swell. Greater poison can lead to decayed flesh, which may result in the loss of fingers or toes. Large amounts of venom can even lead to internal bleeding, which is very deadly.

WHAT TO DO IF BITTEN

- **Seek a healer.**
  Finding a healer is the first thing you should do. Describe what creature bit you and how long it has been since you were bitten.

- **Remove jewelry and tight clothing.**
  The bite will swell, which will be doubly painful if there is jewelry or restrictive clothing wrapped around the infected flesh.

- **Keep the limb still.**
  The more you move the bitten limb, the more the venom has a chance to spread. Keep the infected area as still as possible.

- **Take medicine.**
  There are many medicines that can help with pain, but be wary. Medicine that thins your blood can be dangerous, as it will cause the venom to travel faster.

- **Do not try to capture the creature.**
  There is no need to bring the creature to a healer, and attempts to do so may result in even more bites and infections. However much you may wish for revenge, it is best to leave the beast be.

- **Do not try to suck out the venom.**
  This does not work, and at most it will lead to the venom entering the mouth of another, which will just be a whole other problem to deal with.

- **Do not apply a tourniquet.**
  Some may believe that this will stop the poison from spreading, but it is far more of a hindrance than a help. Cutting off the blood flow will lead to the infected flesh becoming even more damaged.

BLACK MARSH WILDLIFE

Ja'dasha has spoken of the many ways that the swamps of Black Marsh will try to kill you, but what specifically are these plants and creatures? How can you best avoid their dangers and save yourself from harm?

While by no means a complete list, the following plants and beasts are the most notable that Ja'dasha has learned of during her many years of travel.

PLANT LIFE

Not even the plants of Black Marsh are to be trusted, walker. Make one wrong step toward a seemingly harmless plant, and boom! You are dead. To avoid such a fate, Ja'dasha will now list the deadliest plants within the swamps.

As a note, all of these plants can be snuck up on and disarmed by those skilled with the knowledge of how to do so. If you do not have one in your party who possesses such talent, it is best to keep a wide berth.

GAS BLOSSOM

These large, hostile plants release a noxious gas that has been known to kill a grown Khajiit (and other races). You will most likely smell them before you see them, for they are extremely putrid. They must be avoided or disarmed, lest you fall victim to their poison.

STATIC PITCHER

Like the gas blossom, the static pitcher will attack creatures nearby in self-defense. This plant creates a lightning-like charge to strike those close by. Luckily, these plants can be spotted very easily given their eye-catching appearance. Look for thorny vines around the base of the pitcher-shaped plant…and the sparks of energy it emits should also be a clue to you.

LANTERN MANTIS

The most bestial of these plants is the lantern mantis, known for its unusual shape that resembles a certain insect. (A septim to anyone who can guess which insect.) They are prone to strike out with their claw-like appendages at those who pass by.

CATAPULT CABBAGE

The least deadly on this list of plant life is the catapult cabbage, though it is still dangerous. If stepped upon, this curious plant has the ability to propel its victims high into the sky. If these cannot be avoided, it is best to move swiftly past them.

WILDLIFE

If you think the plants of Black Marsh are deadly, just wait until you meet the many beasts that roam the land, as varied as they are dangerous. Here is but a small selection of the creatures you will meet in the swamps, and how they will try their best to kill you.

Usually, Ja'dasha would try to give some advice on how to survive an encounter with such creatures. The truth is, only a skilled warrior will be able to defeat most of these beasts. The best you can do, should you not be a skilled warrior, is avoid them at all costs and run very far away if you see them.

FLESHFLIES

The name of these creatures is not a fanciful one, walker. One fleshfly is no bigger than a grain of sand, its bite annoying but harmless. Its blood-red body is easy to spot as it floats in the air. It is when these creatures swarm that there is cause for alarm, for they will indeed eat the flesh from your bones. Many Imperials (not to mention their horses) have had such a fate befall them as they sought to claim Black Marsh.

Strangely enough, fleshflies do not seek to devour the flesh of Argonians. Ja'dasha is sure there are many theories as to why this is, but she truly does not care. Just know that an Argonian need not fear these creatures … and may need you to remind them that the same is not true for you.

VORIPLASM

Imagine a glob of mucus. Now imagine that the glob is as large as a cart. It is huge and bulbous, without a mouth, but filled with an insatiable hunger. That is a voriplasm.

This creature (if you can call it that) acts purely on instinct. It will grab you and drag you into its gelatinous body and slowly devour you. If the horror this one has described isn't enough, the voriplasm can also form its body into spikes that

pierce its victims. By the moons, we should at least be thankful that it is slow moving and often lurks within the darkest caves of Black Marsh.

It breeds by creating smaller voriplasms from its body. One Argonian claimed that all voriplasms were once a singular body, and that smaller creatures split from a very large mother-beast. If such a tale is true, it is truly one that Ja'dasha wishes to never confirm.

BEHEMOTH

A behemoth looks much like an Argonian, if that Argonian were twice as tall and possessed ten times the muscle. These large lizards cannot speak and know no reason. They will attack any who approach them, defending their territory with a frightening zeal.

As with many creatures with such hulking bodies, their favorite attack is to punch, smash, and otherwise use their large clawed fists to pulverize their prey. They are also known to spit blistering green venom from their mouths, and can summon crocodiles to their side. Ja'dasha does not know if this is because they train the crocodiles or if they just have some sort of pact with crocodiles, but nonetheless it is something to be watchful for.

Oh, and they also enjoy eating Nagas. Ja'dasha's uncle once claimed that he lured away a behemoth by throwing a sack full of dead Naga flesh in the other direction, but this may have been a lie. This one's uncles are fond of telling fanciful tales.

HAJ MOTA

The haj mota are large, shelled creatures with spikes along their backs. They are very territorial, as are most creatures in Murkmire. They are fond of charging their prey, spitting venom on their victims, and stomping them to death. They can also burrow underground and attack you from below. If strength and venom were not enough to kill you, the shock wave that they're able to produce certainly will.

Despite their deadliness, if they can be killed, a delicious stew can be made from haj mota meat, if prepared properly.

WHAT ARE THE HIST?

The Argonians are strange, this is true, but perhaps the strangest thing about them is that their gods do not exist in the sky, nor in Oblivion, nor in another realm at all. They exist within the heart of their villages in the form of the Hist.

This one speaks of the Hist because they are a very important part of Argonian culture. Should you be privileged enough to visit one (and few outsiders are), it is of the utmost importance that you are respectful. Very respectful. Or you will be very dead.

Seeing a Hist, you may believe it at first to be but a very large tree. Some have large trunks while others have long branches, and some are tall while others are wide. Large, glowing flowers cover them like giant torchbugs. Along their bottoms are hatching pools filled with glowing gold sap. This is where Argonian eggs are submerged in Hist sap until they crack and Argonian young emerge from their shell, a birth that allows them to commune with their tree god.

Some say that the roots of the Hist stretch across the entire world. Others say that the Hist are of one mind, their roots entangled with one another. They claim that before man, Mer, and Khajiit, there was only the Hist. This one does not know if that is all true, for many will claim such things about their gods. But this is what many Argonians believe, and so it is wise to nod politely when they speak of such things.

HIST SAP

The Hist speak to the Argonians in many ways, usually through a village's tree-minder. Much like the many priests found throughout Tamriel, these spiritual leaders are highly respected within their tribes. They speak with the Hist through dreams, visions, and even the sounds of the wind through the branches. But the most common way to commune with the Hist is by licking the sap from the tree and receiving visions.

Hist sap is very sacred to the Argonians. It is from this sap that Argonian eggs are hatched, their bodies are changed, and the Hist's will is known. This is to say that it is very, very stupid to try to collect, or touch, or (moons forbid) lick the Hist sap. There are many, many ways to die in the swamps of Black Marsh, but trying to take from the Hist ranks among the most obvious ways to do so.

HIST RITUALS

There seem to be more rituals involving the Hist than there are stars in the sky, for every tribe of Black Marsh has many. From mating to prophesies to war, no two rituals seem to be exactly alike. If you are spending time within a Black Marsh village, it will not hurt to ask about these rituals. Ja'dasha has found that the Argonians are very open with their beliefs, should you be able to decipher their riddle words.

Many of these rituals are not purely ceremonial. Through them, the Argonians are able to strengthen themselves, their scales turning thicker and their magic growing stronger. Some are able to receive prophetic visions of what is to come. Ja'dasha was even part of a ritual where a member of the tribe changed their sex by the power of the Hist! Such a celebration afterward you would think it was a holiday.

Ja'dasha does not like Black Marsh, this she has been very clear about. But there is a beauty in the Hist that even she cannot deny. She does not know if they are gods as the Argonians claim, or if they are even conscious beings. But standing before one, you cannot help but feel that there is a presence before you. Ancient and powerful and strange.

CONCLUSION

Traveling to Black Marsh is a decision that you should not make lightly, walker. It is a land filled with dangers, whether they be venomous beasts or poisonous plants. Muck and mire will cover you head to toe, and many of the local tribes are hostile to outsiders.

But should you brave the swamps, there is a somber beauty to be found. The glowing Hist flowers that light the night sky like red stars in a sea of leaves. The stone monuments of a lost age, coated in moss and lost to time. The croaking of the vossa-satl as it … well, perhaps not the croaking of the vossa-satl for most outsiders. It is an acquired taste.

Thanks to the wisdom of Ja'dasha, you are ready to brave the swamps of Argonia. Moons guide you, walker. You're going to need their blessing.

MORROWIND

Morrowind lies in the northeastern part of Tamriel, and is home to the Dark Elves. It comprises the island Vvardenfell and thesurrounding coastal territory along the west, south, and east of the island. The warm, mild climate frees much of Morrowind from freezing snows, unlike its northern neighbor Skyrim. Other than its climate, the land varies greatly, from rocky coasts to fertile plains to sweltering swamplands. Morrowind's most notable feature is its great mushrooms, which can grow as tall as towers. Some are even hollowed out and turned into houses.

At the heart of Vvardenfell is Red Mountain, a large volcano with fire in its belly and a mouthful of smoke. The surrounding land is filled with lava flows and barren crags, and ash fills the sky and blankets the earth. The smoke and ash are so prominent that the nomads who make their home here are called Ashlanders, and they are just as loathed by the rest of Morrowind as the sooted lands they call home.

The trade in Morrowind is quite lucrative, should you know how to navigate both its land and peoples. And so you have, in your infinite wisdom, purchased Ja'dasha's book! She will not disappoint you, walker, for she has much advice to share.

THE GREAT HOUSES

As you journey throughout Morrowind, it is wise to know which great house owns the land you travel in. First, this will allow you to be aware of the customs, taxes, and trade laws in the region. Second, the Dark Elves, also known as the Dunmer, are very cranky when you do not know. (The Dunmer are a finicky bunch, and this is coming from a Khajiit.)

And so Ja'dasha will give you a quick guide through the many great houses of Morrowind, what lands they own, and some of their customs. Enough for you to get by, for there is much she could speak of and most of it would be very dull.

HOUSE HLAALU

House Hlaalu holds the west-central part of the mainland, as well as southwest Vvardenfell. The strength of their house comes from both business and diplomacy. Unlike many Dunmer, they are happy to negotiate and trade with other races.

They make for good trading partners, should you be careful, for their welcoming smiles hide cunning eyes. It is best to deal with House Hlaalu with a healthy pound of suspicion. Take none of their words at face value, and be sure that your contracts with them are ironclad. Be prepared to grease a few palms and always watch your back should you wish to deal with House Hlaalu.

HOUSE REDORAN

House Redoran controls the western mainland bordering Cyrodiil and Skyrim. The house also recently took control of the northern and western regions of Vvardenfell. Honoring the traditions of the Dunmer above all else, they remain one of the most strict and unchanging of the houses. They are also the largest military power of Morrowind, with many of Vivec's Buoyant Armigers born in the house. They are fair with outsiders, but not particularly welcoming.

They are honest trading partners, should you know how to appeal to their sense of honor. Be sure to show reverence for their ways and admiration for their culture. Know that their word is as good as gold, for they would rather be in financial ruin than ruin their precious honor. Strange, yes, but something that can be taken advantage of, should you be cautious. Double dealings are often dealt with … harshly.

HOUSE INDORIL

House Indoril has dominion over the east-central regions of Morrowind, home to some of the most sacred places within the nation. They are greatly religious, and many hold high positions in the Dunmer's Tribunal Temple hierarchy. They also have a great connection with the Tribunal, claiming to be their loyal servants since they ascended to godhood. If House Redoran is unflinching, House Indoril is made of stone, for they hate change above all else and wish only to keep the traditions of the Dunmer going strong.

This house makes for terrible trading partners and dinner guests, for they speak only of dry, boring doctrine. Ja'dasha has never heard of House Indoril making deals with outsiders. It is best to have a Dark Elf intermediary deal with them, should you find their partnership valuable.

HOUSE DRES

When you think saltrice, you think Dres. The house keeps watch over lands bordering Black Marsh, and possesses the most fertile farms in Morrowind. And with all that farmland, there is always a need for labor, which the House Dres has no short supply of thanks to the slave trade. They are fond of enslaving the Khajiit and Argonians, though their pens hold many races.

They can make lucrative business partners, should you be able to stomach their practices. Be wary, for they may be more interested in your labor than your goods. This one has never ventured into their lands, for what should be obvious reasons.

HOUSE TELVANNI

House Telvanni rules over the eastern region of the mainland and eastern Vvardenfell. They are the most despised of all the houses, even among the Dark Elves. Known for their powerful mages and master wizards, they want little to do with the rest of Tamriel, desiring only solitude and study. Though they have few enemies, they also have no friends, nor do they desire them.

These are horrible business partners, unless you have something that they desire. And even then, House Telvanni is far more likely to simply kill you than bargain for it. It is best to bring a strong force of arms with you should you wish to negotiate with this house, and even then it will be slow going. Telvanni only think of pride and rarely of profit.

ASHLANDERS

The Ashlanders control no territory, but rather live a nomadic life on the island of Vvardenfell. They are allowed to reside only in the most inhospitable regions, and are generally looked down upon by the rest of the Dunmer. This is because they refuse to worship the Tribunal, and instead look toward their ancestors and the Daedric princes for guidance. Likewise, the Ashlanders are not fond of their fellow Dark Elves, and believe them to be weak.

As for trade, why would you even consider the Ashlanders as business partners? They are poor, disliked, and hostile to outsiders. Leave them to their ash.

AVOIDING (LEGAL) ASSASSINATIONS

Tamriel is home to many assassins, but it is only in the lands of Morrowind that such a job is perfectly, completely, and utterly legal in the guild of the Morag Tong—with the constraints that all professions have, of course.

The Morag Tong worship Mephala, and honor her through their murders. Why the Tribunal allows the honoring of a Daedric prince in their lands, this one is not sure. But it would hardly be the strangest thing about the Dark Elves.

To perform an assassination, the members of Morag Tong require a writ. Ja'dasha does not know who writes such writs, nor how the assassinations are determined, but it is very much against the law to assassinate someone without one. To do so means expulsion from the guild, which usually involves being assassinated by another guild member, or so this one hears.

As Ja'dasha writes this, she realizes that she has not much advice about avoiding assassinations. She has never heard of someone surviving the Morag Tong, and is not even sure if it has ever been done. And so she has only one thing to suggest should the Morag Tong receive a writ for your death ... Pray to whatever deity you believe in.

VOLCANO SAFETY

What many would call Morrowind's greatest feature is also its greatest danger. The island of Vvardenfell is home to Red Mountain, a volcano that spews ash into the air and still holds fire within its belly. Though the Dark Elves scoff at such concerns, Ja'dasha is not willing to bet her life on their ease. And so she will tell you all you must know when dealing with an erupting volcano.

PREPARATION

Should you travel anywhere on the island of Vvardenfell, it is best to know evacuation routes should Red Mountain begin to erupt. Familiarize yourself with the location of the nearest road and the nearest port. While you will travel with a good many items, keep essentials in an easy-to-carry pack. This should include water, food, a change of clothing, and any valuables.

Be sure that those traveling with you are also prepared in case of an evacuation. Have a plan of where to meet, what to bring, and what to leave behind. This is especially important to tell both young and elderly travel companions.

PREDICTING AN ERUPTION

The sooner you can evacuate Vvardenfell during an eruption, the more likely you are to survive. And thus it is wise to be wary of the signs that Red Mountain is about to erupt.

As a general note, there may be Dunmer mages who are trained in predicting such catastrophes. However, it is unlikely they will take time to warn outsiders if such a threat is imminent. If there is one thing you can trust about the Dark Elves, it is that they are untrustworthy. So it is best to watch for the signs yourself, yes?

EARTHQUAKES

Red Mountain has been known to cause earthquakes every so often, so it may be difficult to gauge the imminence of an eruption based just on this. But before an eruption, such earthquakes will grow in intensity and number.

HOT AND SWELLING GROUND

The pressure within the earth will cause the land around Red Mountain to grow hot and swell. It may even begin to crack and open in certain places.

STEAM

The mouth of the volcano, and perhaps cracks in the ground, will begin to emit a great deal of steam and smoke.

Unfortunately, all of these things may occur without an eruption, and can happen weeks, months, or even years before a volcano finally erupts. If you happen upon such occurrences on Red Mountain, check with the locals to see if the activity is unusual. Is that earthquake stronger than the ones they usually feel? Is the smoke greater today than yesterday? It is best to be vigilant, no matter how the Dunmer may scoff.

Let us say that Red Mountain takes you by surprise and begins to erupt. Lava will spew from its mouth in a fiery rage, raining boulders and fire down upon Vvardenfell. Ash will begin to fill the skies, choking those who breathe it. Mudflows will ravage the land faster than lava. You must be wary of these dangers, and prepare for them.

STAY INDOORS

If you are a safe distance from Red Mountain, it is wise to stay indoors until the danger has passed. This will help you avoid the many dangers evacuation may bring.

Close all doors and windows, and attempt to cover any other openings. This will help you avoid letting volcanic ash into your shelter. Be sure to bring indoors any livestock or pets that you do not wish to be harmed. They will fare no better than you by breathing in the smoke.

If you believe your shelter to be in danger of collapsing, either from falling debris or rising mudflows, it is best to begin evacuation. Should your shelter remain intact, wait for the eruption to stop and the air to clear before you venture outside. If you or a companion has inhaled smoke, you should seek a healer at once.

EVACUATION

There are many places in Vvardenfell that will not be safe if Red Mountain begins to erupt. In many cases it will be far safer to evacuate off the island entirely. Traveling during an eruption, however, is no easy thing.

MUDFLOWS

Mudflows, as the name suggests, are great avalanches of mud. These are common during eruptions, especially after heavy rains or near stream channels, and can be just as dangerous as lava. They will move far faster than you can walk or even run.

If you are in a valley or lower area, especially if you are near a stream or river, move upslope as quickly as you can. Be sure to look upstream for mudflows before crossing bridges. If you are in the path of a mudflow, move sideways out of its path. This is far more likely to get you to safety than trying to outrun it.

ROCKFALLS

The earthquakes that come with a volcano eruption can create rockfalls, something to be watchful for, especially if you must travel beneath a cliff. It is best to avoid these areas altogether. If you find yourself beneath a rockfall, curl into a ball and protect your head as best you can.

BURNS

Ja'dasha will go into more detail about burns later in this guide, and she will not repeat such advice here. Suffice to say, avoiding being burned is the best way to protect yourself from the dangers of burns. Keep away from lava flows and hot fumes. Hot ash can also burn your skin, so cover your body as much as you can before traveling outside.

If you are burned during an evacuation, it is best to seek a healer as soon as you can.

ASH AND FUMES

The ash and fumes created by a volcano eruption can be just as deadly as the lava that erupts from it, for there is no escaping the air you breathe. Still, there are many ways to mitigate the risks of lung damage during a volcanic eruption.

Eye protection. Protecting your eyes from ash will help with both navigation and unnecessary pain. Though goggles may be an expensive purchase, they can mean the difference between life and death during an eruption. If you have no goggles, seek out any means to protect your eyes from ash that you can.

Masks. The rogues reading this book are in luck, for masks will do you much good during an eruption. They will help keep you from inhaling ash and damaging your lungs. If you have no mask, a damp cloth over your mouth will be better than nothing.

Protective clothing. Wear long sleeves and pants to protect your body from the heated ash within the air.

Avoid fumes. If your nose, mouth, and eyes become irritated from the fumes created by the eruption, it is best to move away from the area as soon as possible. Inhaling fumes may make you lightheaded or weak, which is very dangerous during an evacuation.

Red Mountain may be the marvel of Morrowind, but that does not mean that it is not a very real, very present threat. If you are traveling on the island of Vvardenfell, it is best to be prepared for the worst. Better to be an overcautious fool than a dead one.

THE TRIBUNAL

Of all the races in Tamriel, there are only two who claim to live among their gods. The Argonians of Black Marsh, who grow and tend to tree gods known as the Hist, are one example. The Dark Elves are the other, for they worship three gods known as the Tribunal (or the Almsivi), who live within their cities and rule with absolute authority. On that note, this one does find it rather curious how two races who so hate one another have much in common when it comes to their beliefs.

The Tribunal were not always gods, according to Dunmer lore. They ascended to godhood many moons ago. They do not all look like Dark Elves in appearance. Almalexia still chooses to take the form of a golden Chimer, the race of all Dunmer before they were cursed by Azurah. Vivec has chosen a half form, both Chimer and Dunmer. And Sotha Sil, for reasons all his own, has shared his people's curse and taken the form of a Dunmer. Far be it from this one to speculate on the will of gods, but there is much one can glean from these choices.

Beneath the Tribunal and their absolute power is the Grand Council of Morrowind and the hreat houses. It would appear that these powers are what rule the day-to-day happenings of Morrowind. This one supposes that gods would have little wish to attend to the doldrums of bureaucracy, as they must be quite busy with their divine deeds.

It is not likely that you, as an outsider, will ever meet a member of the Tribunal, much less speak with one. But it is best to know some truths of these gods so that you may best know those who worship them. The Dark Elves do not look kindly on outsiders under the best circumstances, but they will not tolerate those who belittle their gods. And so Ja'dasha will give a quick overview of the Almsivi.

ALMALEXIA

The Mother, the Warden, the Lady of Mercy. There are many names that the Dunmer honor Almalexia with, for she is the most beloved of the three Tribunal. Known for her compassion, kindness, and forgiveness, she protects the weak and is patron to sages and healers. The Mother of Morrowind indeed!

She resides in her eponymous capital of Almalexia, a temple city devoted to worship. House Indoril serves her with unwavering loyalty there. Should you be so blessed, you may actually see her walking among her people in the city streets.

You must never approach her if she walks before you, for her guards will not suffer explanations before cutting you down.

VIVEC

The Guardian God-King presides in the holy land of Vvardenfell in his capital of Vivec City. They say that he is a god of duality, though this may be hard for those not well versed in philosophy to understand. He is a warrior-poet and has written the rather famous 36 Lessons, a set of mysterious texts that none know the true purpose of. For Ja'dasha, this is 36 lessons too many for her to ever read.

One of Vivec's greatest accomplishments was stopping a falling star, known now as Baar Dau, from crashing in Morrowind. This large moonlet now hovers over Vivec City, reminding its people of their god's might and power. It is little wonder why so many pilgrims flood the city each year.

SOTHA SIL

Almalexia walks among her people. Vivec reigns from within his palace. Sotha Sil, however, is the most elusive of the Tribunal. He has more titles than even Almalexia, but most refer to his great mastery of both magic and invention. They say that he rules over the great Clockwork City, hidden somewhere out of reach of most mortals.

The greatest of Sotha Sil's accomplishments, as far as this one is concerned, is the Coldharbour Compact. After the destruction of Gilverdale, Sotha Sil journeyed into Oblivion and met with eight of the most powerful Daedric princes. There he made a pact with them that they would never manifest in Nirn again. There are none who know the details of this pact, save Sotha Sil and the princes he bargained with. But make it he did, and for that we should all be thankful. There is no telling what destruction would be wrought without it.

CONCLUSION

Truly, it is the Dark Elves that provide Morrowind's greatest dangers. Whether it is the slave pits of House Dres or the raw power of House Telvanni, there are far more political dangers within these lands than there are natural ones. And you must navigate both if you wish to survive.

But should you learn to dance with Dunmers, there are many lucrative business trades that can be found here, and a strange beauty besides. The glow of the lava flows during the night is only a little impeded by the ashy air. The towering mushrooms that the Telvanni claim for homes, or the silt striders that carry Dunmers to and fro, are sights not soon forgotten. For a land barren of a friendly smile, there are still many wonders to be found.

And now you can behold that beauty with a far lesser chance of dying before you take your leave, thanks to the wisdom of Ja'dasha. Unless the Morag Tong has a writ with your name on it. That Ja'dasha cannot help with.

CYRODIIL

The Imperial province of Cyrodiil was once idyllic. Located in the very heart of Tamriel, it enjoys temperate climates, gentle countryside, and bountiful woodlands. Mountain ranges can be found to the north and east, though there are many safe routes to travel through them. At its center lies City Isle, home of its capital, the Imperial City. Throughout time it has hosted powerful emperors, bustling trade, and the mysterious White-Gold Tower.

Indeed, Cyrodiil was once a lovely land to visit. The Empire had sturdy roads, guarded outposts, and many wondrous cities filled with the latest comforts. Many merchants were happy to travel in the Empire, assured that both their wallets and their lives were in good hands. That was only until recently, however, when the land became ravaged by war and covered in Daedric forces.

As it stands, no moon-fearing traveler would dare to set foot in Cyrodiil at the moment. And so Ja'dasha's advice for journeying in Cyrodiil is quite simple: Do not do so! Choose another path, another kingdom, another journey. At least until Cyrodiil knows peace once more.

HIGH ROCK

Far in the northwest of Tamriel, High Rock is a land of isolated valley towns and rugged highland strongholds. Rather than follow one absolute ruler, the land is instead divided into a variety of city-states and minor kingdoms, each with their own government. And while this independence suits the Bretons of High Rock just fine, it can make for some tricky politics when the province must act as a whole.

Compared to much of Tamriel, the Bretons are quite welcoming to strangers. This may have to do with their own mixed heritage, for every Breton boasts both the blood of Mer and man. Here you will find tournaments honoring noble knights, taverns packed with boastful bards, and festivals filled with singing and dancing. Should the Bretons not be on the brink of civil war once again, that is.

The terrain of High Rock shifts from windy crags to temperate forests, rolling badlands to snowy mountains. This can make for varied travel, so it is best to plan your route carefully before heading to High Rock. And while the land may not be treacherous swamps or deadly deserts, there are still dangers that lurk within these kingdoms.

But have no fear, for Ja'dasha is here to ensure your survival with her wisdom.

FINDING YOUR DIRECTION

Traveling will do you little good if you do not know where you are going. And while there are many roads to Daggerfall, there are also many ways for one to get lost. So it is best to find your heading and keep to it, yes?

READING A MAP

Maps are created with the intention of guiding travelers to their destination. Without them we are lost, yes, but they hold little use for those who cannot read them. How can you best choose, read, and care for your maps? Let this one tell you.

CHOOSING THE BEST MAP

There are two types of maps you can choose from. The best map for you depends on where you are traveling and what sort of terrain you must traverse.

Road Map. These are maps that are crafted to display constructed roads. They are excellent resources for traveling on common trade routes.

Physical Map. These maps focus on natural features and terrain, such as rivers, lakes, terrain, and footpaths. These are best for traveling through locations that have no major roads.

Ideally, one would have both types of maps with them as they travel, for you never know when a horde of atronachs may block a major roadway. But for those on a tight budget, it is wise to choose the best map for your traveling needs.

THE RIGHT SCALE

The larger the scale of your map, the less area it covers. This may seem counter-intuitive, but think of the size of a common map. If the scale of every feature on it is very large, then there will be less space for the map to continue onwards. So which is right for you?

Large-scale maps. These maps contain far more details with far more accuracy, but cover less terrain. This may be necessary for traveling in a particularly hazardous location, such as a mountain, or in an area you are less familiar with. It is also nice to have if you are able to afford several maps.

Small-scale maps. These maps contain less detail but cover far more area. This is good to get a larger sense of the land you are traversing. It also allows you to purchase and travel with fewer maps, as they cover more terrain. For journeys you are familiar with, or those less hazardous, this may also be all that you need.

As this one said before, it would be best to carry both large- and small-scale maps with you. One map could cover the entirety of your trip, while several more can focus on specific locations throughout your journey. After all, one wouldn't want to confuse Hag Fen for Cambray Pass. This of course all depends on your budget and storage space … and the availability of the maps.

THE LEGEND

Ja'dasha speaks not of epic tales now, but rather the legend of a map. This is sometimes also referred to as a key. The legend lists the symbols and lines drawn on the map and tells you their meaning. These descriptions will often be written in shorthand, so as to not crowd the map with too much text.

Unfortunately, different map makers will use different symbols on their maps. It is good to familiarize yourself with the legend of a map quickly. One can also buy maps from the same mapmaker in order to ensure having legends with consistent abbreviations.

Here are some common considerations one must have when reading the legend of a map.

Paths. Familiarize yourself with what types of paths are indicated on your map. You will need a wide, clear road if you wish to travel by caravan. However, travelers on foot may find an easier route with footpaths. Remember that not every path will be marked on your map, so it is always wise to keep track of distinctive landmarks as you travel.

Symbols. Symbols are very useful for landmarks that are otherwise difficult to draw directly on a map, such as towns or cities. These often help you keep track of your direction. They can also tell you what type of lands you will travel through, such as a temperate forest or bog.

Abbreviations. There is nothing clearer than the written word when it comes to directions, and abbreviations can help clarify symbols. These can also give names to important landmarks, such as ruins or temples, allowing you to know what to expect upon arrival.

FINDING YOUR LOCATION

This is easier said than done, especially if you lose track of your surroundings. Thus it is good to keep track of what landmarks you have passed by and to keep a careful watch for what landmarks you should expect to see soon. Whether it be the Beldama Wyrd Tree or Mire Falls, there are many such landmarks to mark your path through High Rock. As always, the best way to find your way is to never be lost at all.

If you do end up lost, try to find any major landmark that you can orient yourself with. Bodies of water, such as rivers and lakes, work wonderfully for this, as they should be clearly marked on your map. Halcyon Lake is one such example in High Rock. Mountains are helpful as well, for they can be seen from a great distance. Finding a town would be excellent, as you can simply ask the locals where you are.

As a general note, this one has found Bretons to be especially welcoming, and they are always willing to point you in the right direction. Aldcroft serves particularly good ale, ported in from all over Tamriel. Crosswych is a great place for new horseshoes, as the blacksmiths are excellently trained in such arts. And Daggerfall has a little of everything, being the largest city in High Rock. And it has the largest price tags, too.

It is also wise to carefully plan your route and note how long it should take you to arrive at certain destinations. This will take research on your part, such as seeking the knowledge of those who have taken your path before. How many days does it take to travel from this river to this town? How many weeks in total should your trip be? This is also important when planning how many supplies to bring as well.

ORIENT YOUR MAP

Your map will be of little use if it is turned wrong side up! When you are confident that you know where you are on your map, look for what features are ahead, behind, and to either side. For example, if there is a prominent lake in front of you, you can face the map in the same direction. This is especially important if you must move around landmarks and cannot follow a straight path.

CARING FOR YOUR MAP

A map will do you little good if it is sogging wet, torn to pieces, or burned to a crisp by an irate mage. Thus it is wise to carry your map in a safe location at all times.

The best way to carry a map is in a leather map case. This cylindrical case should be waterproof and easy to seal tightly. Some come with a strap for ease of travel, for many travelers choose to keep their maps on them at all times. Otherwise it should be stored in a safe location in your caravan or travel packs.

Be gentle as you unroll the map, to avoid tearing or creasing it. Be sure to hold it in your hands or place it on a clean, dry surface when surveying your location. Be sure that it is out of reach of young ones and fools who may mishandle it.

USING A COMPASS

Just as essential as a map is a compass to show you north from south. However, Ja'dasha has met with some truly dull claws who knew next to nothing when it came to navigating with such a device. And so she imparts her wisdom so that you will not torture your traveling companions as this one has been so tortured in the past.

Unlock the compass. Some compasses possess a mechanism to lock the needle in place. Be sure to unlock it before starting to navigate.

Place on a flat surface. The needle of a compass is most reliable when the compass is lying on a flat surface. This can be a table, cart, box, or whichever, so long as it is flat.

Try the center-hold technique. While less reliable, one can master the technique of holding a compass so as to get a true reading. Open the compass so that both base and cover are completely flat. Fold one thumb above the base of the compass, and one below. Place your fingers along the side of the compass. Stand with your elbows tight at your side and your compass held in front of your stomach.

Match north. Slowly turn your compass so that the needle that points north is aligned with the section of your compass housing labeled north. Simple.

Align with the map. Shift your map so that it correctly faces north. From there, place your compass on your current location and draw a line (physically or mentally) to your intended destination. This will tell you which direction you must head.

Be careful of false readings. If you are in a location with a lot of metal, such as a cart full of armor, then it may affect your compass's reading. Try moving to a different spot.

Watch for broken compasses. Compasses are prone to becoming damaged. Be sure that your needle is able to move freely within the compass, and consistently points in the same direction. If concerned it might be damaged, check the bearing with another compass that you are sure is in working condition.

Keep in a safe location. Just like your map, a compass is not an item you want to lose or break. Be sure to keep the compass where it is easily accessible but not prone to being dropped, lost, or otherwise ruined.

HORSE RIDING

Horses are a much-needed part of any merchant's travels, providing quick means of transport and a way to ferry goods over land. We Bandaari live by our pedlar steeds, dressed finely and well suited for long travel. In High Rock you'll find everything from the absurdly strong coalsmoke forge horses to the hardy witch knight chargers. Truly, the steeds of Tamriel are just as varied as its kingdoms.

However, there are many issues and even dangers that can arise from such a method of traveling. What can you expect to go wrong? How can you best meet these challenges? Listen to the wisdom of Ja'dasha.

Ja'dasha has no advice for those who choose to travel on strange mounts, such as silt striders or bears. For such specifics you must consult another guide.

CARING FOR YOUR HORSE

Should you be fortunate enough to afford such a fine thing as a horse, you should also be wise enough to care for the creature. It is best to avoid injury, exhaustion, and even undue stress. A happy, healthy horse makes for smooth travels.

Health evaluation. Before leaving on your journey, it is best to check that the horses you plan to bring are in pristine condition. If you are not wise in the ways of horse health, it is best to seek the wisdom of one who is. Most stable masters will be happy to provide this service, and their advice is well worth whatever fee they may require.

Horseshoeing needs. A horse bred for travel will most likely be fitted with horseshoes most of its life. Just as you must carefully decide on footwear while traveling, you must also do so for your horse. Studs may be needed for slippery terrain, or pads for rocky paths. It is best to discuss your traveling plans with a farrier beforehand, so that they may recommend the best horseshoes. They can also evaluate if your horse needs its hooves trimmed, or new horseshoes, before heading out. Better to prepare beforehand than have your horse throw a shoe on the road.

Medical supplies. Bring emergency supplies in case your horse is injured during travel. Items such as large bandages, medications, ointments, and any reading materials you may have on the topic of horse health would be wise. Store these together and make sure all of your traveling companions are aware of their location.

Regular rest stops. A horse used to travel can move at a trot for a good portion of the day. However, it is best to rest your horses at regular intervals and allow them to graze and drink water. This is especially important if you notice that your horse is growing exhausted. Be ever watchful for the following signs:

Slowed pace. As with most creatures, a horse will choose to go slower to ease their burden.

Decreased responsiveness. A horse will be slow to respond to commands to turn and stop as they become more exhausted.

Unwillingness (or inability) to increase speed. This may be due to exhaustion rather than stubbornness.

Reduced coordination. Your horse may begin to stagger, sway, or run into obstacles it would otherwise be able to avoid.

Increased head and neck movement. While this may seem as if your horse has an itch, increased movement may be another sign of exhaustion.

Heavy breathing. As with you and Ja'dasha, an exhausted horse will begin to breathe heavily.

Should your horse be exhausted, it is best to take a break as soon as possible. An exhausted horse is far more prone to being unresponsive to commands, unable to increase speed, and will be clumsier while traveling. A short rest will waste less time than a horse with a broken leg.

FOOD AND WATER

Horses should be offered water throughout the day at regular intervals, which also allows for regular rests. Try to water your horse every three to six hours if possible. This is also a good time to allow your horse to graze.

As for how much food to provide your horse, this depends on many factors. How large is your horse? How far are you traveling each day? Is there vegetation for the creature to graze upon? Should you feed your horse hay, or is grain better? It is best to consult an expert on such matters before heading out. Ja'dasha recommends a stable master for such wisdom.

As for a feeding schedule, it is much like our own. Feed your horse their meals every morning, afternoon, and evening. This can match your own eating schedule.

CONSIDER TERRAIN

Different horses are better suited for different terrains, which is only common sense. A creature that has spent its life on desert sands may find it difficult to walk upon rocky paths. Thus it is wise to consider what terrains your horse is used to and if they will face challenges along the way.

This consideration can be avoided by renting or purchasing horses that have been trained in the land you are traveling through. However, if such a thing is not possible, it is best to adjust to a slower traveling speed to give your horse time to adjust. Be observant and watch for signs of exhaustion or struggle. This is particularly important in rough terrain, such as mountains, deserts, swamps, and so forth.

THROWN HORSESHOES

A thrown horseshoe can cause a host of issues. Here is how to handle such a crisis.

Prevention. Be sure that your horse is regularly seen by a farrier and fitted with new horseshoes. Be sure to hire a farrier of good reputation. They are worth their weight in horseshoes. And be careful of muddy terrain.

Evaluation. Check the horse's foot as soon as you notice that it's thrown a shoe. Assess if the hoof is damaged or if there are still nails embedded. If part of the horseshoe remains, it is important to pry it off. Thus it may be wise to keep farrier tools on hand.

Keep weight off the horse. A horse without a shoe is prone to injury, pulled muscles, and bruising. It is wise to not ride the horse until they are evaluated and reshoed.

Seek a farrier. Most towns should have someone wise in the way of horses, especially in High Rock, where they are fairly common. Have the farrier evaluate the hoof and reshoe if possible.

Allow time to heal. If the horse is injured during the process of throwing a shoe, it is best to give them time to heal. A farrier's advice should be followed in such an event.

Just as you must care for a cart, boat, or any other means of travel, so too must you care for your horse. Take note of their struggles and ease their burdens, and your travels shall be far smoother for it.

THE ORCS

Many merchants dread the thought of bargaining with Orcs, thinking them violent and untrustworthy. This is foolish thinking, for the Orsimer are a people rife with tradition and laws, just as any other culture in Tamriel. While many find their ways barbaric, the Orcs believe themselves to be stern yet just. They have a proud and long tradition of exceptional blacksmithing, and their warriors can hold their own against any Redguard or Nord.

The Orcs hold claim to small pieces of land throughout Tamriel. Some live in clans, while others make their way to cities or large towns in search of work. The largest stretch of land held by Orcs is Orsinium, a city-state in High Rock.

STRONGHOLDS

Traditionally, Orcs live in strongholds led by a chieftain. The chieftain is the only male allowed to take wives and father children. Any other male within the tribe can challenge the chieftain for his position, but must kill him by fair combat to take his place.

The chieftain takes many wives, some of whom will hold special titles. The forgewife is in charge of all blacksmithing and armory. The hearthwife is in command of all domestic duties, such as cleaning, cooking, and sewing. The shieldwives act as protectors of the chief. The elder women of the stronghold, generally mothers of the chieftain, are known as wise women. They hold the duties of healing, both physical and spiritual.

While the chieftain's sons train for the day they will kill their father, the chieftain's daughters are often traded away to become wives of nearby chieftains. There is always a choice, however, and many stronghold children will join armies, become mercenaries, or take up blacksmithing in a nearby town or city.

RELIGION AND TRADITIONS

The Orcs worship Malacath, the prince of curses and oaths. It is said that long ago the Orsimer were once elves who followed the divine being known as Trinimac. One day, Boethiah swallowed Trinimac and excreted the being known as Malacath. This transformed both the deity and his followers into Orcs, cursing them as outcasts.

Many Orcs take pride in their status as outsiders and pariahs. They believe this brings them closer to their god Malacath, who is patron of the spurned and ostracized.

The Orcs also honor the Code of Malacath, a set of unwritten laws that is passed down by the wise women of strongholds. This code prescribes consequences for unneeded violence, theft, and other transgressions, which is a price rather than punishment. This can be compensation in the form of gold or goods, but can also be paid in blood.

A blood price can be far more literal than first thought. The offending party has the right to shed the blood of those who have wronged them until satisfaction is met. Some clans literally weigh the blood spilt! As one may suspect, this can, and has, led to deaths. Such is the Code of Malacath.

This one's advice, if you have broken said code? Offer every septim, every good, even the shirt off your back before you offer your blood. For you will not enjoy the process by which they extract.

CITY-ORCS

Many Orcs seek a life in cities and towns, and thus are known as City-Orcs. They are often looked down upon by Orcs who live in strongholds and are considered to have grown soft by this choice. Generally, City-Orcs will choose to live by the traditions of wherever they have made their home. For example, you can expect the Orcs of Daggerfall to be as friendly as their Breton neighbors.

CONCLUSION

From friendly Bretons to stern Orcs, from misty crags to lush forests, the land of High Rock is a patchwork of experiences. Visit any town, and you may find yourself swept up in a grand festival. Dare to approach an Orc stronghold, and you will find weapons andawarriors beyond your imagination. Adventure awaits around every corner, should you be brave enough to explore it.

And while this may seem exciting to many, these adventures can come with some unexpected struggles. From navigating to your destination to ensuring that both you and your horse survive the journey, there is much to consider when traveling along these roads. It is only by being prepared for the unexpected that you shall live to travel another day.

And prepared you are, thanks to the many words of Ja'dasha.

VALENWOOD

You have not gazed upon a true forest until you have stepped in Valenwood. Called Tamriel's garden by the Imperials, there is truly no better way to describe this tropical land, which is filled with traveling trees taller than city buildings and covered in lush, green plants as thick as Skyrim's snow. You will find this coastal kingdom nestled in the southwest of Tamriel, with warm weather befitting such a location. But unlike the arid heat of Hammerfell, the warmth of this forest is unusually humid, so much so that breathing in the air at times can make one feel that they are drowning on dry land.

While some think Valenwood to only be filled with jungle, there are many varied regions in the kingdom. To the southeast lies the dense woods of Grahtwood, home to Elden Root, the capital city based around a giant elden tree. To the southwest is Greenshade, consisting of smaller forests, clearings, meadows, and even swamps. To the northwest lies Malabal Tor, a jungle region even denser than the woods of Grahtwood. Here lies Silvenar, said to be the spiritual center of Valenwood. To the northeast is the region called Reaper's March, where the Northern Woods diminish as they merge with Elsweyr's savannas.

It is in the Northern Woods that the Bosmer make their home. Small and nimble, the Wood Elves reject the more civilized (some would say haughty) nature of their High Elf and Dark Elf cousins in order to find harmony with nature. They live a simple life among the trees, adorning themselves with beast teeth and leathers. But do not mistake this simple life of the Wood Elves for a life led by those with simple minds, for the Bosmer are quite cunning as well. There are many who are prominent scholars and traders, as well as scouts and thieves.

THE GREEN PACT

So in tune are the Wood Elves with the forest that they never take from its bounty, refusing to use wood and plants to feed or clothe themselves. They live a simple life among the trees, only eating meat and drinking naught but water and milk. Even their alcohol is made of milk and meat juices, a vile drink known as rotmeth brew. (Yes, they ferment such vile liquids just as we Khajiit ferment sweet moon-sugar cane. Ja'dasha wishes to speak no more of this.)

This life is not simply a choice for the Bosmer, but rather a deeply rooted belief known as the Green Pact.

It is believed that the deity Y'ffre first created the forest, known to the Bosmer as the Green. She gave the Green the power to shape itself, and this was known as her first tale. After this she created the Wood Elves, who had the power to tell stories. This was her second tale. So in love with her creations, she warned the Wood Elves to never change their shape and never change the shape of the Green. Transforming their bodies and destroying the forest were strictly forbidden.

Instead of taking from nature, the Wood Elves were granted the power to ask for its aid. Thus they could ask the forest to shape itself to their liking, such as creating shelters from living roots. In return, the Wood Elves protect Valenwood with a religious fervor, and do not take kindly to those who would seek to destroy their Green.

And thus we come upon our first survival tip for Valenwood.

CANNIBALS

As part of the Green Pact, the Wood Elves use only creatures to clothe themselves, create their tools, adorn their homes, and nourish their bodies. They believe that not utilizing every part of a slain beast is sinfully wasteful. All of which, while unique to Valenwood, are hardly dangerous practices worth noting in a survival guide such as this.

But horrifyingly, there are a small number of Wood Elves who apply this logic to their fallen foes. After all, are not you and Ja'dasha creatures of a kind? And that certainly is worth noting in this guide, this one thinks!

Yes, there are Wood Elves who will consume your flesh and make tools of your bones should you make yourself an enemy of them. Any enemy they slay, be it beast or Mer or Khajiit, will be used in such fashion. And thus we see why many merchants try their best to avoid Valenwood. For it is one thing to die on your travels, and entirely another to be eaten as supper shortly afterwards.

Ja'dasha will note that these Wood Elves (supposedly) do not revel in the act of cannibalism, but rather feel that it is their duty to not waste that which could be useful. This act is only done after killing another by way of battle or in an act of self-protection. Thus you will not find yourself hunted for sport, as many claim. Most of the time.

A few tips to keep yourself from ending up on a Bosmer's menu:

Tread carefully. Many Wood Elf tribes watch over the expanse of Valenwood, and some are more welcoming to visitors than others. Be sure to carefully plan your route to avoid territorial tribes.

Hire a guide. There are no better guides through Valenwood than the Wood Elves that were born there. Hiring a guide to help you traverse the land is always a wise decision, and doubly so when dealing with cannibals.

Keep to the Green Pact. Many Wood Elves do not take kindly to the destruction of their forest, intentional or otherwise. While within Valenwood, try to keep to their customs. Do not take from the forest, lest you be taken in turn.

MEAT ON THE MENU

In many parts of Tamriel, you can purchase foodstuffs from the many towns you come across during your travels. And while there are Wood Elves who would be happy to sell you their wares, you may find these friendly villages to be few and far between. Not to mention the uncertainty of these purchases. Is that cut of meat from a creature? Or from kin? There are many who would rather not take such a chance.

Thus it is prudent, perhaps more so than in any other kingdom, to be prepared to hunt for your own supper.

HOW TO HUNT

While there are many who spend their entire lives mastering the art of hunting, it is a skill that anyone can learn. Here are a few tips to get you started.

Be prepared. By this time, you have learned Ja'dasha's mantra that being prepared is the most important step. Be sure that you have the correct supplies, know your travel route, and check the skies. Hunting in the rain is far trickier than hunting during clear weather.

Scout the area. Take the time to walk around an area to learn its pathways, clearings, waterways, and so forth. This will give you a better idea of where animals may rest to graze or drink, and where you can lie in wait.

Mask your smell. The creatures that you hunt are extremely sensitive to smells. It is prudent to cover your scent so that you blend into the forest. In Valenwood it is common practice to use mud, blood, and other very disgusting things to cover one's scent. One other common and less disagreeable way to mask your scent is to take common plant matter, such as pine needles or cedar leaves, and crush them in your palms. Then rub the resulting powder or juices over your clothes. Best to crush leaves that have already fallen from their respective trees, so as not to violate the Green Pact. (At least Ja'dasha is fairly certain this does not violate the pact. Feel free to consult a Wood Elf friend if you doubt her.)

To avoid such nonsense, you can (and should) bring common oils along with you. If you don't already have such oils, you can purchase them from local tribes or traders.

Choose your spot. Much of hunting entails patiently waiting for your prey to come to you. Thus choosing the right spot to lie in wait is of extreme importance. Ridges will give you a good vantage point to spot your prey. The corner of a field or clearing is also an excellent location, as this is a common entry point for prey creatures. The intersections of natural forest paths are also good, as many animals will use the paths throughout the day.

After choosing where you believe the animal will appear, always be sure to hide yourself downwind of the location. This will help mask your scent.

While there are many obvious spots to hunt an animal, these may be highly contested by other hunters. This is doubly so within the forests of Valenwood, where the Wood Elves depend so heavily on hunting. What some might deem a potentially bad location for hunting, such as a ravine that's tricky to navigate, may end up being more bountiful than a prime location.

Above all, no matter where you choose to hide, be sure that you are lined up for a clear shot. A hunter will usually only have time to loose one arrow before the animal is alerted. Be sure to make that first shot as accurate as possible.

Be silent. Just as many creatures have an incredible sense of smell, so too do they have excellent hearing. Try to be as quiet as possible as you travel through the forest. If you *do* make a sound, try to stay as still as possible for a good length of time after. This will give any creature you are hunting time to settle back down after being alerted to your presence.

Avoid footpaths. While traveling through Valenwood is far easier by finding and using footpaths, your scent in these areas may alert prey to your presence. The Wood Elves avoid such troubles by traveling through the treetops, but unless you are a Bosmer or Dagi, it is most likely that you will travel along the ground. Try to take the road less traveled to further hide your presence.

Know thy prey. The more you know about your prey, the better chances you will have to catch the creature. When do they travel? Where do they prefer to go? Many prey animals will travel during dusk and dawn to avoid predators such as you. Thus you may find yourself forced to wake up quite early in the morning or waiting long into the night to find your prey on the move. Such is the rugged life of the hunter.

Expect a long wait. Hunting requires patience, especially given that many prey creatures will sleep for most of the day to avoid predators. It is prudent to be prepared for a long wait. Be sure to bring food and water with you, and choose a spot that is comfortable. You will most likely be there for some time.

Making the kill. You spot your prey, shoot an arrow, and hit the creature. Excellent! But often that is only the start of the hunt. Many wounded creatures will not stay down and wait for you to finish them off. They will run and you must follow.

Keep track. Knowing where the animal was located when hit is important, especially if you are quite a ways away. If the animal drops to the ground, you must know where to locate it. If the animal immediately runs, this will be where you start the chase.

Let the creature run. Chasing a creature will only spur it on to run faster and farther than it would if not chased. Wait a good while before tracking down your prey.

Approach carefully. Even if an animal appears dead, it may simply be resting. It is best to make noise or throw a rock away from the creature to see if it startles and rises up again. That way you can track where it moves next.

Look for blood. Tracking the animal often involves looking for blood trails along the ground, rubbed against tree trunks, or even speckled on leaves. The blood will begin to thin over time, making the trail harder to follow. Keep looking!

End it quickly. When the creature is found, be sure to end its suffering quickly and efficiently. This will often involve slitting its throat or piercing its heart. Keep a steady hand and offer a prayer, for this animal's life was taken for yours to continue.

Know how to field dress. Cannibalism aside, the Wood Elves are right in that no life should be taken so that the meat should rot. Learning to dress your prey quickly will keep it from spoiling. This is an art in itself, and is best learned from a skilled hand rather than a guide such as this one.

GONE FISHING

The forests of Valenwood are filled not only with creatures to hunt, but also with rivers, streams, and lakes to fish in. And while fishing may be a true test of patience, even compared to hunting, it can also be far more appealing in many ways. This is especially true for those who may find the practice of hunting rather grisly.

Still, fishing requires more than patience to master. Here are a few tips to get you started.

Equip yourself. A fishing rod, line, and hooks are the most important supplies you can carry. Steel hooks are best, given their durability against rusting. A bucket will help keep your fish alive, especially if you desire to keep bait fish. A net will help land any fish you reel in.

As this one said in her hunting advice, field dressing fish will help keep the flesh from rotting. A knife to gut the fish and a rope to tie them up will help ensure successful transport to your cooking fire.

As may be obvious, cooking fires are a tricky thing with the Green Pact. While the use of coal and peat are allowed, these may not be available to you. In which case you can eat your fish raw, or you can pray that no Bosmer comes upon your cooking fire. Take your pick.

Bait your hook. There are a number of different ways to acquire bait. Local markets may sell lures created from metal, wood, threads, and other materials. These items will mimic the look and shimmer of small fish and insects.

A cheaper way is to catch live creatures that larger fish want to feast upon. Insect parts, worms, crawlers, and fish roe are all excellent for this; you can use anything you can push a hook through. Smaller fish, known commonly as bait fish, can be caught with a net before you start fishing in earnest. Minnows and shad are commonly used. It's best to keep these fish in a bucket so they can stay alive during the course of the day.

Choose the best location. Where is it best to cast your line? Shady spots, especially where the water is deep and cool, are particularly excellent for hot days. Fish enjoy a respite from the hot midday sun, just like you and this one. This is preferable for fisherfolk as well, as they need to keep cool as they await their next catch.

Deep, calm pools of water are more likely to hold fish, especially in active streams. You can also look for eddies of water, which form near rocks that create a swirling movement in the water. This current brings in insects, and so it's a good place for fish to lie in wait for their next meal.

If you are fishing near the shore of the ocean, reefs are an excellent spot for fishing. These are paradises created by coral and rocks where fish like to gather. These may be deep under water and hard to spot, but the local fisherfolk can point you in the right direction.

Land or boat? Fishing from a boat is best for lakes, oceans, and large rivers. The larger the body of water, the more likely the fish will be found farther inward.

For those of us fishing in smaller bodies of waters, or who have no boat, it is fine to fish from land. Try to find banks, sand bars, or piers that are close to the water. You can wade into the water to reach deeper pools and eddies. This is also a lovely way to cool down during hot weather.

Choose the right time. Midday means heat, and fish are less likely to feed while the sun's highest in the sky. Thus it is better to fish during the cooler dawn and dusk hours. These are also the times of day when insects are spawning and active, which means that fish are more lively and looking for a meal.

If you are fishing in the middle of the day, it is best to use bait that imitates live fish and can sink lower in the water. This is because fish are less likely to come to the surface and eat bugs during the afternoon. Bait fish are also good to use at this time.

CASTING YOUR LINE
Many believe fishing to be as simple as putting a piece of bait on your hook and plopping it into the water. These fools couldn't be more wrong.

Before casting, make sure that you let out enough line to throw your hook far into the water. Use the weight of the hook and lure to push it out away from you so that it can be cast out farther than you can naturally throw. Aim up and out in order to cast as far away as possible, and then flick the rod so that the line shoots forward.

This is far more complicated than it sounds. It is far better to learn how to cast your line from a fellow fisherfolk before attempting the technique yourself.

If you are in a boat and very wise (though some may call you lazy) you can try trolling. This is a technique where your fishing line is drawn through the water while the boat drifts slowly across the water, which means that you do not have to keep casting your line, as it will move along with the boat. Trust Ja'dasha on this, your casting arm will thank you.

FLY FISHING

Fly fishing uses a lightweight lure, so that the line can float on top of the water. The lure is generally created from small twigs and bird feathers, with the intent of mimicking the look and motion of certain insects, frogs, small fish, or the like.

When fly fishing, you must mimic the pattern of a live insect or fish with your lure. Cast your line out as far as possible over the area where you believe the fish are to be found. You then use a technique known as stripping line. This involves pulling the line in little bursts so that it jerks the lure through the water to imitate a floating or swimming creature.

WHAT TO AVOID

As with hunting, it is best to hide your presence from your prey while fishing. This means keeping quiet and not creating vibrations in the water. Try not to speak loudly, rock your boat, move your legs, or throw items into the water. This will scare the fish away.

It is also important to be aware of what creatures may be in the waters that you fish, or what lies in the branches above you. Fishing can be a relaxing pastime if not disrupted by a giant spider or territorial salamander! Be aware of what creatures may be fishing for you before casting a line.

Though more a courtesy than a fishing technique, it is thought to be rude to fish near someone else, especially in close quarters. If a fisher has already claimed a fishing hole, it is polite to move to another location. Be quiet and cautious as you do so, as you do not want to scare away the fish they are attempting to catch.

Last, it is best to be aware of the local laws and abide by them. Where is it legal to fish? Are there certain fish you must throw back? Trust this one, you do not want to catch a trout in someone's sacred lake. It causes far more trouble than it is worth.

WISE FISHING PRACTICES
While this advice will do little to help you catch fish today, it will ensure that your children can catch fish tomorrow.

Release immature fish. It is common wisdom that you should throw back smaller fish that have yet to grow to their full maturity. This ensures that the fish will grow old enough to spawn and continue their line. Likewise, catching only larger fish not only ensures a full stomach but also ensures the local fish population remains healthy. The small fish need to thrive in order to feed the larger fish, which then in turn flourish and feed us.

Move to different locations. Continuing this thread of thought, it is best not to overfish in one area, and instead rotate where you fish. This also allows fishing populations to remain healthy. You should also not fish during spawning seasons, so the fish have time to lay their eggs and ensure the next generation. If you are unsure what areas are safe to fish in, be sure to ask the local fisherfolk. They will be keeping track of such concerns.

WATER WORRIES
Any traveler worth their moon-sugar knows that it is best to bring fresh water with them. Whether this is carried in casks, barrels, flasks, or waterskins, it is important that water is always kept on hand. Every town and city is an opportunity to use the local well to fill your water supplies before heading out once more.

FINDING WATER
While mages can conjure fresh water from thin air with their alteration magic, we mundane folk must make due with our wits and our survival guides. What do you do if your water supply runs out? How can you find water, and what is safe to drink? Ja'dasha will teach you.

Listen. Running water sources, such as rivers and streams, are actually quite loud. This is a double blessing, for running water is often safe to drink as well.

Search downhill. Water tends to run downhill, so follow valleys, ditches, and gullies. Find your way to low ground and you should find your way to water.

Follow animals. Animal tracks, insect swarms, and even flying birds can help lead you to water. After all, they need to drink too.

Check tree and rock crevices. Any indent found in nature, no matter how small, may contain small pools of water. However, this water is often unsafe to drink and may need to be cleansed first.

Collect rainwater. Rainwater, especially in areas such as Valenwood, can be collected for drinking. It is best to do this in an open area, for rainwater can still be unclean if it drips from trees, houses, and the like. It is also time consuming to collect.

Collect morning dew. For the truly desperate, collecting dew in the early morning is possible. Tie cloth around your ankles and wade through dew-covered grasses and plants, then wring out the water. Just be sure the dew wasn't clinging to something poisonous!

Rely on fruits and vegetables. While many plants do not hold a good deal of water, they can still help satiate thirst. Be careful in Valenwood, however, for the Green Pact looks down on such practices.

WATER TO DRINK

You have collected water. Excellent! Now, is it safe to drink? Consuming foul water can lead to a host of issues, such as vomiting, diarrhea, and fever—all symptoms that lead to a greater loss of water than what you have taken in. So how do we know what water we can drink?

SIGNS OF CLEAN WATER

The water comes from a running source. Running water sources, such as rivers and streams, are best to drink from. Collect water upstream whenever possible. The farther you are from the mouth of the river or stream, the better.

The water comes from underground. Though often trickier to find, these sources of water are clean as well.

The water is clear and tasty. Water that is free of particles, and has a pleasant taste and smell, is usually safe to drink.

Other creatures drink it. If other animals are drinking from the water, it is often safe for you to drink from as well. Be cautious, however, for many creatures are made of sterner stuff than us.

SIGNS OF FOUL WATER

The water is stagnant. The smaller the body of water, the dirtier it usually is. Think of a muddy puddle versus a clear stream. However, this can also be true of ponds and even lakes. They can still be filled with detritus, debris, plants, and even small creatures!

The water is unclear and foul tasting. It isn't hard to tell if water is unclean. It is often brown and brackish, and has an unappetizing smell and taste. If you are unsure, have a small taste of water before gulping it down.

Beware of liquids other than fresh water. In desperate times, some may be tempted to drink any liquid that they can, even such things as urine, sweat, blood, and seawater. These are extremely dangerous to drink even in the direst of circumstances. They all contain high levels of salt, and will do more to increase your thirst than help it. They may even make you ill.

CREATING DRINKABLE WATER

If all you have on hand is foul water, there are many ways you can ensure that it is clean for drinking.

Let the water settle. Dirt, detritus, and the like will settle to the bottom of an immobile container of water over time. Collect the water in a vessel and then let it lie still for some time, until the water at the top of the container appears clear. This clear water can then be used for drinking.

Boil the water. This is often best done in combination with letting the water settle. Take the clearest water you can and heat it to boiling. This will make the water far safer to drink once it has cooled.

Use cleansing magic. If you should be blessed with a mage on hand, they may have cleansing magics to clear the water. Some merchants even sell powders that can cleanse water for you, though these should only be purchased through reputable sources, such as the Mages Guild.

CONCLUSION

Valenwood is indeed the garden of Tamriel when it comes to its lush plants and deep forests. Plants the colors of jewels, trees as tall as towers, and so much more await you if you choose to travel in these forests. And while not every Wood Elf tribe may be welcoming to outsiders, this one has found many to be gracious hosts. Take the time to hear the tales of their spinners, listen to the rhythm of their leather drums. You may even wish to try a tankard of rotmeth brew should you be truly brave (or truly stupid).

But just like any other land in Tamriel, Valenwood must be treated with respect and met with preparedness. Whether it is avoiding a tribe of cannibals or hunting for your next meal, there are many things to consider before starting your journey in these forests.

The Green may welcome you into its arms, but will it be willing to let you go? Luckily, you are now swift and quick and wise thanks to the wisdom of Ja'dasha.

SUMMERSET ISLE

It is said there is no kingdom as beautiful as Summerset, island home of the Altmer. Summerset's warm climate is perfectly matched by the island's colorful forests, home to trees with leaves of green, pink, and purple. You may chance upon the stately indrik while traveling through its elegant meadows, or come upon a majestic griffin as you hike through the island's mountain crags. The natural beauty of Summerset is well matched by the wonder of its cities, for each brick and building seems torn from the pages of a fantastic fable.

The High Elves who call Summerset home are just as stately as their island. From their appearance to their households, everything is meticulously manufactured to be of the highest quality possible. This fastidiousness is equally met by their magical prowess, for there are few in Tamriel who can boast of feats of the arcane like the High Elves. Why then are not the streets of Summerset filled with crafters, traders, and mages from around the world?

This is because the High Elves detest outsiders more than any other race in Tamriel. According to them, if you are not Altmer, you are not worthy of the splendors of Summerset. And so, even on an island so perfect and picturesque, those who dare to land on its shores are still in need of survival tips. Trust Ja'dasha on this one.

MAGIC AND MAGES

While magic is present throughout Tamriel, nowhere is it more celebrated and integrated into everyday life than Summerset. And thus it is prudent that all who wish to enter the Blessed Isles are aware of the fundamentals of this powerful art.

SPELLCASTING

Magic can be performed in a number of ways, but the most common is spellcasting. This is the ability to use your own magical reserves to change the world in some manner. No two mages cast magic in quite the same way, but there are common schools of spellcasting that you can become familiar with.

Destruction. As implied, these spells are meant to destroy and harm their targets. This can either be done through pure magical force or by commanding the elements. If you wish to corrode, hinder, or weaken a foe or object, this is the school for you.

Restoration. This school of magic represents the opposing force to destruction: magic that heals, mends, and strengthens its target. It is through these spells that armor is mended, poisons are rendered inert, and fevers are healed. Mages skilled in restoration magic are wonderful traveling companions, as they can greatly aid in many survival situations.

Conjuration. This type of magic is the act of summoning otherworldly creatures to aid you, often Daedric or undead. These guardians are loyal to their mages and are often summoned to protect them in battle. This magic can also be used to summon Daedric armor and weapons, as well as banish Daedra back to Oblivion.

Alteration. These spells can alter the physical or magical properties of the target. Some examples include making an object lighter, giving someone the ability to breathe underwater, and granting elemental shields. Many mages regard this magical school as holding the greatest possibilities.

Illusion. The spells of this school play on the perception of a target. They can create a false appearance for someone or something, and can also charm, excite, and calm a target. This type of magic is also able to grant invisibility, illumination, night vision, and so forth.

Mysticism. The strangest school of magic, mysticism deals with the manipulation of magic itself. Many scholars debate the nature of this school of magic, and many more fear it, given its ability to manipulate souls. Some even compare it with necromancy. Some uses of these spells include reflecting damage, absorbing spells, and even trapping souls in objects.

Thaumaturgy. While thaumaturgy does not change the appearance or nature of an object, it can change the laws of reality temporarily. This includes levitating objects, walking on water, and even short-range teleportation.

ALCHEMY

Alchemy is the act of combining ingredients to create magical potions and poisons. This can be done through mixing, boiling, or distilling ingredients such as plants, animals, and even bits of Daedra. Unlike spellcasting, there is no innate magical skill needed to perform alchemy. This means that the art can be learned by anyone.

A truly great alchemist can create potions that heal instantly and poisons that kill just as quickly. While potions are often drunk to take effect, weapons can be coated with a poison to make them even deadlier.

ENCHANTING

Enchanting is the art of augmenting weapons, armor, and other items with magical properties by imbuing them with the power of a soul. This is almost always done with the power of a soul gem. In general, the more souls used to power the object, the more powerful it will be. Over time, the power of the enchanted item will diminish and more souls will be required to continue its enchantment.

There are many enchanted items created by the Aedra and Daedra that have been gifted to Nirn. These are the greatest enchanted items in existence, far more powerful than any mere mage could possibly hope to achieve. It is the dream of many adventurers to come upon one.

OTHER MAGIC

While far too numerous to be included in this guide, there are many other forms of magic. Necromancy is perhaps the most well known, being the ability to raise and control the dead. Auramancy evokes memories and emotions. Weather magic can manipulate the rain and wind. There's even cheesemancy, though this one is uncertain of what uses there are for that.

Just as there are endless ways to perform magic, so too are there endless studies about it. And the leading experts on such matters can be found in the Mages Guild.

THE MAGES GUILD

Those who wish to learn more about magic, or perhaps become a mage or alchemist themselves, must apply to join the Mages Guild. This professional organization is spread all throughout Tamriel and is devoted to the teachings and further study of magic. The guild is led by the arch-mage and the Council of Mages, who decide guild policies.

Local guilds are required to help the general public by addressing magical concerns, selling alchemical ingredients and potions, and teaching spells. Most guilds are keen to take on new recruits and teach the next generation of mages. Each guildhall also holds a large collection of magical texts and tomes, often with a portion of the collection available to the general public.

RECOVERING FROM MAGICAL ATTACKS

Not everyone has command over the magic of restoration, but all of us can understand the basics of healing. Summerset is home to the leading authorities in such matters, and thus it is only natural that Ja'dasha speaks of such matters in this section.

This one has already spoken of wound care, poisons, and venoms in earlier sections of this guide. Here she will focus on wounds commonly acquired from magical attacks.

Spells can bludgeon or cut the same way that hammers and swords can, but there are many ways that a mage can harm you that no warrior could replicate. Below is a quick list of common magical wounds and how you may tend to them.

As always, any serious injuries should be tended to by a healer.

FIRE MAGIC

A fireball is a favorite attack by mages, as it is easy to perform and easier to spread. One well-placed fireball can leave a horde of enemies on their knees. This is a good topic to cover, as one can receive burns from nonmagical ways as well.

TREATING SERIOUS BURNS.

Serious burns can be identified by the following signs:

The burn is deep. The deeper a burn is, the more dangerous.

It affects a large area. The area a burn covers is as important as how deep it goes. Any burn larger than a closed fist may require a healer's care.

The skin is charred. Blackened skin is not a good sign when it comes to either burns or frostbite. The skin may also have large patches of white or brown.

If you or a companion has serious burns, there are steps you should take before acquiring the aid of a healer.

Protect from further harm. Move the burn victim away from the source of the damage, whether it be a campfire or an angry mage.

Check for breathing. Make sure that the victim is still breathing and alive. This will save you unnecessary healing expenses. (Or, if you are proficient, you may attempt to prompt their breathing once more.)

Remove restrictive items. Remove anything that may be covering the burn, for the flesh will begin to swell. Remove anything around the neck to allow for easier breathing.

Cover the burn in cool cloth. A clean, cool, and moist bandage will help with the pain and keep the wound clean.

Elevate the burn. If possible, raise the wounded area so it is higher than the person's heart. This helps with the circulation of magical energies. (Or blood, depending on the scholar.)

Watch for shock. Shallow breathing, a pale complexion, and fainting are all signs of shock. This is not a good sign and raises the urgency of finding a healer.

Avoid treating with water. It may seem best to douse the burn with cool water, but this can lead to hypothermia, which is very bad (as this one discussed previously).

TREATING MINOR BURNS.

A minor burn does not require a healer's attention. These burns can be diagnosed by the following signs:

Slight redness. Similar to a burn one may receive from the sun, a minor burn will be slightly red and slightly rough.

Minor pain. Minor burns still hurt, but not nearly as much as severe ones.

Blisters. The skin may blister with even minor burns, but this does not mean that it is serious enough to need a healer's attention.

A small affected area. Minor burns will cover a smaller portion of the skin than severe burns.

While a minor burn does not require the attention of a healer, there are still ways you should go about treating it.

Cool the burn. Apply a cool, water-soaked compress over the burn. This will help with the pain.

Remove items around the area. Just like severe burns, minor burns will swell. Remove rings, jewelry, bracelets, or any other items on or near the burned area.

Apply salves. When the burn has cooled and is no longer hot to the touch, there are a number of lotions and salves that can relieve pain and promote healing.

Bandage the area. Cover the burn with a loose gauze, avoiding putting pressure on the skin. This helps reduce pain and protects blisters from being punctured.

Take potions (if needed). Pain-reducing potions can be taken, if you have some on hand.

Leave blisters alone. Do not agitate or break any blisters that have formed. If they are broken, apply a healing salve.

SHOCK MAGIC

Like burns, injury from shock damage does not always require immediate aid from a healer. Here are signs that the victim of a shock spell should be tended to by a professional.

Severe burns. Luckily for you, Ja'dasha has already covered this in a previous section.

Confusion. If the victim is having trouble speaking, understanding speech, or is otherwise disoriented, this may signify a serious injury.

Difficulty breathing. Shock damage goes deeper than flesh, and can sometimes cause the victims to lose the ability to breathe. This is a bad sign. Seek immediate help.

Muscle pain. If the victim's muscles are contracting in painful ways, this is a sign that the injury is quite serious.

Fainting. A bad sign for any injury!

Here are a few steps you should take if a companion is on the wrong end of a shock spell.

Avoid immediately touching someone affected by shock magic. Some shock spells will last quite a while, and you will be of little help to your companion if you become injured as well. Be sure that all shock magic has left their body before assisting them.

Do not move the victim. Unless your companion is in immediate danger, it is best to bring a healer to them rather than risk further injury by moving them.

Care for burns. Shock magic can produce burns just as fire magic can. This one has already covered this topic in detail in a previous section.

Keep the victim warm. A chilled victim of this magic may go into shock. Keep them warm.

FROST MAGIC

Frost magic can induce hypothermia, frostbite, and all manner of cold-related injuries. However, Ja'dasha has covered these topics in detail previously. Refer to those sections if experiencing injuries from frost magic.

There are many more ways a mage can harm you, including damage to your mind or very soul. These are outside of Ja'dasha's realms of expertise, however. Please consult a healer, spiritual leader, or Mages Guild representative if you are worried about such things.

THE FUNDAMENTALS OF CAMPING

One would expect to never require camping equipment in the civilized nation that includes Summerset. This picturesque island is filled with towns, cities, and taverns all within a short distance from one another. What need have you for tents and campfires?

That is unless you're a Khajiit, and suddenly the inns all seem to be filled and the taverns are suddenly no longer serving supper. Such was Ja'dasha's experience when she first visited Summerset. Never had this one expected that she would have to sleep outside and cook her own meals! And so she trudged off to a nearby clearing just as the cloudy skies began to open. Joy upon joys, she would have to sleep in the rain.

But Ja'dasha was not the only traveler who had been denied a room that night. By a moons-blessed chance, this one would come upon an Orc who had met the same fate. Her name was Urza, and she took pity on poor Ja'dasha and offered to share her camp for the night. This one happily accepted, though it would soon become clear that she knew not the first thing about camping in the wilderness.

And so Ja'dasha shares with you the very first lessons she learned that fateful night, huddled beneath a canopy of purple leaves on a warm Summerset night.

CAMPSITE SETUP

Finding the perfect place to camp for the night is just as important as setting up the camp itself. Here are the important features to look for:

Flat and clear land. A flat area will ensure that your cart does not roll away in the night. Likewise, a space clear of roots, rocks, and other obstructions ensures that your equipment and bedrolls will be well settled.

High ground. The higher the better, excepting the tips of mountains. This will keep rainwater from pooling at your feet, and benefits from a breeze to keep away insects.

Nearby trees. These can provide protection from the rain, wind, and sun, all excellent things to be shielded from while camping.

Nearby water. As Ja'dasha noted previously, easy access to water will be of great benefit to you when it comes to drinking, bathing, and cleaning.

Now that you have chosen a perfect spot, how can you best set up your camp?

Keep it organized. Knowing what equipment is where can ensure that nothing gets lost or left behind. It is also wise to keep track of how many supplies you have left.

Find a spot for rubbish. Scraps of food can attract animals and should be disposed of away from the camp. Other rubbish should be collected in one spot and properly disposed of. This is especially important in Summerset, for the Altmer do not take kindly to those who dirty their island.

Set up extra tents. Though a luxury, any extra tents you have can be used to store equipment and protect it from the elements. This also helps keep the tent you are sleeping in clean and open.

CREATING A FIRE

What good is a campsite without a cozy fire to keep it warm? Here is some advice for setting up a campfire.

Choose a safe location. Fire burns things, as you may already know. Thus, your fire should be a good distance from your tent, dried leaves, trees, and other objects that may catch on fire.

Be prepared to douse the fire. Keep a bucket of water (or sand) on hand to quickly douse the flames if needed. Use a shovel to pile dirt on top to smother the embers. This is especially important if you need to leave quickly or hide your presence.

Choose good firewood. The best firewood is branches that have long since fallen from trees and are already dried.

Collect tinder and kindling. A fire requires both tinder and kindling to burn. Tinder is easily burned items, such as dry leaves, small twigs, and grass. For kindling, use smaller sticks to start your flame and larger ones to keep it going.

Create a fire ring. Many campers use a circle of large stones to keep their campfire contained.

Follow these steps to build your campfire:

Pile the tinder. The tinder is where your campfire shall be born. Pile it at the very center of the fire area.

Add small kindling. Place small pieces of kindling on top of, but not directly pressing on, your tinder. This formation looks much like a small pyramid or mountain of wood covering the tinder.

Ignite the tinder. Use a long match or ignited stick so as to not burn your fingers. A small fireball, if a mage is available, is also a good choice (remember that Ja'dasha said small).

Feed the fire. Keep adding tinder and small kindling as the flames grow in size. You can also gently blow at the base of the campfire to help it grow.

Add large kindling. Once your flames are adequate, it is time to add your larger sticks to the fire to allow the fire to maintain itself.

A campfire is useful for keeping you warm, allowing you to see during the dark nights, and for cooking meals. Safely creating, maintaining, and dousing a campfire is a skill every traveler needs to know. And now you do.

PREPARING AND COOKING MEALS

Often you will find yourself preparing meals while camping. Here are a few tips on how to safely do so.

Keep foodstuffs safe from beasts. While a cart can be safely packed, those traveling on foot will find that their food supplies attract animals. To prevent your campsite from being targeted, place your food away from your camp and tied up in a tree. This will prevent creatures from disturbing your camp and stealing your food.

Store food properly. Your provisions will be of little use if they become moldy or contaminated, or are consumed by insects or vermin. Make sure that your foodstuffs are stored properly and in the proper containers.

Cook downwind. The smell of roasting food can attract animals. Try to cook downwind of any known animal dwellings to prevent this.

Watch for burning. Cooking over an open flame can be a fair bit trickier than using one's stove at home. Keep watch over your food while it cooks, lest it burns and you go to bed hungry.

CONCLUSION

Summerset is truly a paradise to those who are welcomed to its shores. From picturesque glades to meticulously crafted cities, there is no end to the luxuries that this island has to offer. While there is magic to be found in every kingdom of Tamriel, none quite compare to the charm of Summerset. If you are a High Elf, that is.

But for those of us who are not so welcomed, there is still plenty you should be prepared for when you visit this so-called Blessed Isle. Perhaps you will be the soggy Khajiit who is unexpected and unprepared for her first journey away from home. Or perhaps you will be the kindly Orc who offers a tent to share.

The choice is yours, walker. Make the wise one.

THE DAEDRIC PLANES

While this guide was created to introduce the dangers of Tamriel, Ja'dasha would be remiss not to add a section on the Daedric planes. While these realms do not technically exist in Tamriel, or in our world altogether, many travelers have unfortunately made their way into one over the course of their adventures. And so this one feels that she must share her wisdom, however limited it may be.

Know that the rules of our world need not apply within the Daedric planes. The impossible suddenly becomes very much possible within these realms, often in horrific ways. Each plane is ruled over by a Daedric prince, a powerful deity whom many compare to a god. And as with most gods, many princes have devoted worshippers who join together in cults.

Daedric cultists can be found throughout every kingdom of Tamriel. Whether it be the boisterous Nords, the enigmatic Argonians, the forest-loving Wood Elves, or the stoic Redguards, there is no race nor city that is completely free of the Daedric cults. And with these cults comes the very real threat of being forced into one of the many Daedric planes, most of which are nightmarishly dreadful.

But Ja'dasha is getting ahead of herself. To understand how to survive against these cultists, one must first learn about the deities they worship, yes? So let us begin with that.

A PRIMER ON DAEDRIC PRINCES

There are many Daedric princes to speak of, and they go by many names. Ja'dasha will refer to them by their most common name, for every race has their own interpretations. She must also note that there are Daedric princes who seek to protect and guide Tamriel, though they are few and far between. Even they, however, can be dangerous if vexed.

✹ AZURA

Known as Azurah to the Khajiit, Azura is a benevolent prince. She reigns over dawn and dusk, and all the magic that twilight holds. She also holds dominion over magic and mystery, fate and prophecy, and vanity and egotism. Above all, she wishes for our love, and for us to love ourselves. This leads to a deep devotion from her followers.

Azura lives in her realm of Moonshadow, a realm so beautiful it is said to leave mortals half blind. She rules from a rose palace in a city of silver, covered in flowers and pastel trees. Should you venture into her realm, she is said to be most welcoming. She may even gift those who earn her favor with a most powerful relic, the Twilight Star.

We Khajiit hold a special love for Azura. She is the mother of our people, crafting our beautiful forms in the shape of her own. She gifted us moon-sugar, sweetest of foods, and knows the name of every Khajiit who walks upon the sands. When we pass from this life, it is to her realm we venture, for there lie the Gates of the Crossing. There she will lead us to the Sands Behind the Stars. Should we be worthy.

✹ BOETHIAH

Also called the Prince of Plots, Boethiah earns her title well. Ruling over the spheres of deceit, conspiracy, treason, and assassination, she is a Daedra to be feared. She cares only for blood spilled through conquest and battle. Her followers will often battle each other to the death to earn her favor. She is often known to incite bloodshed, whether by offering trials or by her powerful plotting.

Little is known to Ja'dasha about Boethiah's realm, known as Attribution's Share. It is said to be a country of betrayals and labyrinthine policies, covered in maze

THE DAEDRIC PLANES 153

gardens and twisted towers. To be sure, it is a dangerous realm to find oneself in, for Boethiah is to death as sweet is to sugar. If you earn her bloody favor, she may grant you her Ebony Mail, granting its wearer great protection against magic and physical blows, quiet movement, and a poisonous aura.

✹ CLAVICUS VILE

Although he's known as the Prince of Trickery and Bargains, you would be surprised by how many come to Clavicus Vile to fulfill their wishes. They always are granted what they ask, but never receive what they truly desire. It is said that Clavicus Vile does this not out of spite nor malice, but rather out of boredom from his endless existence. For what better pleasure than seeing one seeking their deepest desires, only to be granted their greatest despair?

Clavicus Vile rules over the Fields of Regret, a land of tranquil country and cities of glass. By his side is Barbas, a shape-shifting Daedra who often takes on the appearance of a hound. Win Vile's favor, and he may see fit to gift you the powerful Masque of Clavicus Vile. This relic is said to make its wearer unbearably charming. A fitting power granted by one who so often deceives with venomous promises.

✹HERMAEUS MORA

The Lord of Knowledge is said to be the wisest of the princes, and certainly has knowledge beyond any mortal. His appearance is frightening to behold, even among Daedra, for he chooses the form of a many-eyed being with no true shape, merely swirling darkness. Some claim that Hermaeus Mora can read both past and future as easily as you read this guide.

The prince lives in Apocrypha, an endless library that contains all knowledge. The books have no titles, and it is said the souls of scholars haunt the many stacks. Here is kept forbidden knowledge, unknown and unknowable to mortals. Show yourself to be wise enough and Hermaeus Mora may grant you the Oghma Infinium, the Tome of Power.

✹ HIRCINE

Known as the Lord of the Hunt and Master of Beasts, Hircine is a prince who many pray to, even if he does not seek such worship. He cares only for those who can master the skill of the hunt, and will often challenge mortals to seek and kill difficult prey. He is also said to be the Father of Manbeasts, and many were-creatures call upon his guidance for their blessing, or curse his name for their affliction.

Hircine rules over the Hunting Grounds, an endless forest filled with both skilled hunters and deadly prey. Those who worship Hircine are said to enter this realm when they die, allowed to live out an endless hunt. It is here that the Great Hunt is held, where a host of hunters chase after the hunted party, known as the hare (which is often not a hare). Should they be the first to slay the prey, they are said to be granted Hircine's boon.

Though perhaps not as powerful as a boon, the prince has gifted his favored followers with the Ring of Hircine. This relic will temporarily grant the wearer the gift of lycanthropy, with complete control over transformations. A lycanthrope who wears this ring will also gain control of their transformations, and no longer be affected by moons or bloodlust.

⦿ MALACATH

As the God of Curses, Malacath is certainly not a prince you wish to vex. He is patron to the ostracized, and holds domain over both curses and oaths. Once a divine deity known as Trinimac, he was consumed by Boethiah and excised from her body. This not only transformed him into a gruesome prince, but was also said to transform his Elven worshippers. We know these followers today as the Orcs.

Malacath rules over Ashpit, so named for its ashen lands and smoke-filled air. In the center of this realm is said to lie the Ashen Forge, filled with iron towers and endless longhouses. It is there to which the Orsimer believe they will journey after death, where they can eat their endless fill and fight an endless fight. Those who Malacath finds worthy may be awarded Volendrung, the Hammer of Might. It is said to sap the strength of the foes it strikes and give that power to its wielder.

⦿ MEHRUNES DAGON

There is no Daedra so hungry for battle as the Prince of Darkness and Destruction. He holds dominion over destruction, change, revolution, and ambition. It is said that when his cultists call upon him, earthquakes and storms rage, so strong is his desire for chaos and carnage. Before the Coldharbour Compact, Mehrunes Dagon was known for destroying entire cities on a mere whim.

We may be thankful that Mehrunes Dagon is now bound to his realm, the Deadlands. A land of destruction and constant change, it is filled with streams of lava, pools of sulfur, and constant storms. Those who please Mehrunes Dagon with their destruction may be gifted Mehrunes' Razor, a powerful ebony dagger that can kill any foe instantly.

MEPHALA

The Lady of Whispers holds influence over the spheres of murder, lies, sex, and secrets. Quite a range of specialties for one prince to hold, but hold them Mephala does. Also known as the Webspinner, she takes great interest in the affairs of mortals, often pulling threads in their web of their interconnected lives and consequences, and weaving deceptions. Above all, she and her followers value mysteries and secrets.

Mephala's realm is the Spiral Skein, a world of dark caverns and crawling spiders. The realm is covered with tall towers, red crystals, and luminous mushrooms. Earn this prince's favor, and she may grant you her Ebony Blade, a relic of great evil that steals the life force of the victims it strikes. Those who wield it can absorb their foes' power and make it their own.

MERIDIA

Known as the Bright Lady, Meridia controls the realm of light and life. Unlike her prince siblings, she is known as a deity of benevolence because of this. Her hatred is reserved for the undead and the necromancers who control such beings. She can even grant those who follow her with immortality, though this comes at the cost of free will. These immortal servants, known as the Purified, serve her without question. It is said such a gift is also granted to those who have defied her.

Meridia's realm is the Colored Rooms, which is as bright as the light that the prince commands. However, it is difficult to grasp much more than that from tales told. Some say that the realm resembles coral, while others report it is nothing more than floating stones. The ground seems to be covered with luminescent water that can be walked upon.

Meridia may gift those who earn her favor with Dawnbreaker, a glowing longsword that can smite the undead.

✸ MOLAG BAL

Controlling the realm of domination and enslavement, there is no prince who desires the souls of mortals more than Molag Bal. It is said his hunger is so great that his realm has swallowed entire sections of Nirn to satiate him. Those who are sacrificed to him are endlessly tortured for his amusement. He is the most dreadful prince, and his cultists often sacrifice themselves to their lord to please him.

Molag Bal rules over Coldharbour, a cold and lifeless realm filled with tortured souls known as the Soul Shriven. In Coldharbour you'll find dark reflections of the mortal realm, monuments to Molag Bal's cruelty. It is also said that the souls of vampires enter this realm upon their demise. Earn this dark prince's favor, and he may grant you the Vampire's Mace. This relic can trap the souls of the mortals it strikes.

✸ NOCTURNAL

As the Mother of Shadows, Daughter of Twilight, and Lady Luck, it is little surprise that many of the thieves of Tamriel call upon Nocturnal for her favor. Her realm is the sphere of night and darkness, though many also believe she holds sway over luck. It is said she claims herself to be the eldest of the princes, born from the void before even Oblivion.

Nocturnal's rules over the Evergloam, a realm of perpetual twilight. The sky is filled with a purple hue, and the world is covered in twisted forests and crumbling monuments. Crows and ravens fill the branches, some even granted the power of speech. The greatest of Nocturnal's gifts is the Skeleton Key, able to open any door. It is a relic that is highly prized among thieves.

✸ SANGUINE

It is easy to see why many would wish to worship Sanguine, the Lord of Revelry. His sphere is related to debauchery, hedonism, and dark passions. Though never intentionally cruel, Sanguine's many pranks and fantastical parties can lead to much trouble for we mere mortals. It is said that those who drink from the prince's goblet can never leave his celebrations. Fortunately, many do not wish to.

Sanguine holds control over many smaller realms, known collectively as the Myriad Realms of Revelry. It is thought there are a hundred thousand of these planes of existence, and each is fashioned from the desires of those who visit

them. As such, the prince actually has little control over these realms, which is just as he prefers.

Those who please Sanguine may be gifted his Sanguine Rose, which has the power to summon a lesser Daedra. While the Daedra will not harm the one who summoned it, it cannot be controlled in any way. This makes the relic far less desirable than other princely prizes.

✹ SHEOGORATH

While many princes delight in chaos, it is Sheogorath who controls the sphere of madness itself. Known as the Mad God, it is said that his motives are inscrutable. He often ends up causing trouble for mortals, torturing those who gain his interest in truly bizarre ways. As such, there is no reasoning with him, for the ways to defeat him are often as insane as the prince himself.

Sheogorath rules the realm of the Shivering Isles, and every mortal who enters this plane will eventually become insane. The realm is split in half, with one side known as Mania and the other as Dementia. These two realms represent the prince's split personality, and the two sides of his madness.

Gain the favor of Sheogorath (and do not ask how, for no one truly knows) and you may be granted the Wabbajack. This staff has the power to turn any one object into another, completely at random. For instance, it may turn a mighty foe into a harmless rabbit. On the other hand, it may turn that foe into an even more powerful creature. One could expect no less from the relic of the Prince of Madness.

DAEDRIC CULTS

Daedric cults worship one of the many princes, and it is the desires of this prince that drive their every action. In return, they hope to be granted fortune, fame, and power beyond the means of any mortal. The ends of these cultists are often tragic, for many of the princes are fickle deities indeed.

Many cultists openly worship their prince, such as the Ashlanders who worship Azura, and are despised in their homelands because of this. Others are far more akin to priests than cultists, such as those who worship Azurah in Elsweyr. The Morag Tong celebrate murder by assassinating in the name of their god, Mephala, and their actions are protected by law. Daedric worship is certainly seen differently by various cultures, kingdoms, and princes.

Ja'dasha would be remiss to not mention the largest cult that currently plagues Tamriel, the terrible Order of the Black Worm, who worship Molag Bal. You will have no doubt heard of their dreaded dark anchors that threaten to pull Tamriel into Coldharbour. Or perhaps even seen one, moons have mercy on your soul.

Most cultists worship their prince in secret, and for good reason. Many live on the outskirts of society, so that they may worship without interference, however their prince may demand so. This worship generally involves murder, torture, and sacrifice. And for such things to be done, they need unwilling victims.

It is these cults that shall cause the most of your troubles as you travel, for the princes themselves generally do not take interest in common travelers. We shall leave them to be dealt with by the powerful and adventure seeking. Besides, there is little advice Ja'dasha could give you anyway if you *did* catch the attention of a prince.

SURVIVING A CULTIST

So what is one to do if they are met with a cultist? Let us consider the possibilities.

As with many of Ja'dasha's survival tips, the best way to survive a dangerous encounter is to not encounter it at all. This is very true for cultists, for preparation can go a long way to making sure you are not the one chained to the table when it is time for a sacrifice.

Travel in groups. Cultists, like bandits, often target those who are isolated and weak. The larger your traveling party, the less likely you are to be targeted.

Stay in towns. Camping may save you septims, but it holds a danger greater than beasts and monsters. Cultists will often strike during the dead of night to gather their victims. Try to rest in inns as much as possible as you travel.

Trust no one. A poor spinster tells you, come quick! Her husband is injured! Do not be so quick to follow, walker, for she may be a cultist luring you toward a trap.

Escape at any cost. If you have read Ja'dasha's previous discussion of abductions, you will remember that she was very cautious in advising you to escape. The dangers of escape attempts far outweigh the benefits, lest you know that your captors meant to kill or sell you.

Cultists wish for one thing, and that is sacrifices for their princes. They may kill you outright or perhaps in a gruesome ritual. They may even use your corpse as a host for a Daedra, so that the creature may walk in Nirn unknown. And so, with all your might, with all your power, you must escape from a cultist. Even if it may cost you your life. Death is far better than what awaits you..

DARK RITUALS

Let us say that you could not escape, and the cultists have begun to perform a dark ritual. There are several ways for you to tell that such a ritual is occurring, which means the urgency for escape has escalated tremendously.

Strange symbols. This one does not expect you to be fluent in Daedric script, but there is no mistaking its twisted letters. These symbols will be drawn upon the floor or wall in large circles, often using blood or some other such horrible substance.

Bitter herbs. Daedric princes must truly love the most bitter of herbs, for their followers burn it with a fervor during their rituals.

Glowing crystals. As with most magics, cultists will often use crystals, soul gems, and the like to perform their dark rituals. These will often glow a frightening color, like crimson, dark purple, or sickly green.

Ritualistic chanting. Usually spoken in Daedric or ominous riddles, these chants are performed to summon Daedra or ask a favor of their prince. It may sound similar to a prayer, which this one supposes it is.

When you are the victim of a dark ritual it may seem that the end is in sight. And that is mostly true, Ja'dasha supposes, but there are some things you may still try to do.

Escape. This is most likely impossible, but perhaps you are truly clever, or luck is on your side. Never stop watching for an opportunity.

Beg. This will not help, but it may make you feel better. Possibly your pleading will stir the conscience of a newer cultist and grant you a quicker death.

Pray. May your deity of choice have mercy on your soul.

ESCAPING A DAEDRIC REALM

In a cruel twist of fate, those who are sacrificed by Daedric cults often find their souls trapped within a prince's realm of Oblivion. And not often the nice realms of Oblivion. Do not expect to see rose palaces or golden saints.

And so Ja'dasha will outline the steps one can take after entering a Daedric realm, whether sent there by cultists or by some other means.

Assess your mortality. There are many ways that a living mortal may enter a Daedric realm, but far more ways a deceased soul may enter it. Assess if you are alive or if you have truly perished. This may be fairly difficult but should be attempted anyway. Here are some signs that you may be a wandering spirit:

- Transparency
- Glowing
- Lack of hunger or thirst
- A sense of mortal dread

Observe the realm. Which realm you have entered will vastly change how you are to survive. Take note of the geographical features, comparing them to the details you have memorized from this book. A cavern filled with spiders? Welcome to the Spiral Skein. A dark wood filled with talking crows? You have entered the Evergloam.

Find friends. You will likely not be the only one to enter this haunted realm. Try to find other mortals and form a group. With luck, one of you may even find a warrior or mage who can defend against attackers.

Avoid enemies. While a mere mortal will be beneath a prince's notice, the Daedra that lurk in the realm will certainly take note. Try to avoid them at all costs, especially if you are still alive. It is unlikely you will survive an encounter.

Gather information. While the survivors you find may not be the most coherent, they will have information for you to gather. Where are safe locations? How have others possibly escaped? Whatever information you can collect from those trapped in the realm may prove helpful.

Keep calm. This seems impossible to do, for by the moons you are trapped in a Daedric realm! But as with all survival techniques, panic will get you nowhere. Stay logical, stay focused, and above all stay calm. There have been many mortals who have escaped the Daedric realms. You can be one of them.

Find a way out. The method will be different for each realm. Usually you want to find a portal leading back to the mortal realm. This can perhaps be summoned by a powerful mage, or be a natural occurrence in the realm. They do exist, and they can be found. Just try your best.

Be alert for opportunity. There have been reports of princes granting boons to those who win their favor, but this is a rare occurrence. One such example is winning Hircine's Great Hunt, a feat that few can claim. Still, it is worth pursuing if you think you can please the particular prince whose realm you're trapped in.

CONCLUSION

Tamriel's dangers do not end with bandits and monsters. Oh no. Most horrid of all are the dark Daedric cults that plague every kingdom of this continent. Devoted to powerful princes, these cultists are always on the lookout for their next sacrificial victim. Whether it is escaping a cult's clutches, or even surviving in a Daedric realm, this guide has advised you of your best options for survival.

However, let us be honest. There is little we can do when faced with the might of Oblivion, should we not be heroes of legend. And so, as with all survival tips Ja'dasha has shared, the best course of action is to never have to survive such an ordeal at all. Stay safe, stay vigilant, and stay cautious. Your life very much depends on it.

FAREWELL AND SAFE TRAVELS

And so you have read all the wisdom that Ja'dasha has to offer when it comes to surviving the many lands of Tamriel.

Or perhaps you have skipped to the end of the guide, which is a very strange choice. Just as there are many adventures that await you, so too are there many dangers. Being prepared to face such situations is the very first step to surviving them. You have of course realized this, or you would not have purchased this wondrous guide.

And perhaps you will share this knowledge with others, just as the kindly Urza shared her knowledge with this one. Tamriel is large and wonderful and terrible, and much more besides. Together we can make it a little less dangerous for all of us.

That is all. Ja'dasha has no more wisdom to share, and her paws grow very stiff with how much writing she has done. Farewell, walker. And safe travels.

ABOUT THE AUTHOR

Tori Schafer is a writer and narrative designer for video games, and she has worked on titles such as *Elder Scrolls Online and Spellbreak*. Her love of games is matched only by her love of tarot, which she has been practicing since she was a child. When she's not playing games or reading tarot, she's spending time with her husband and beloved, bratty cat in their city apartment.

ABOUT THE ILLUSTRATOR

Erika Hollice is a Chicago-based illustrator who loves incorporating a touch of fantasy in her art. Her work draws influence from contemporary and classical artists alike, and is heavily infuenced by her background in game art.

NOTES

NOTES

Published by Titan Books, London, in 2024.

TITAN BOOKS

A division of Titan Publishing Group Ltd
144 Southwark Street
London SE1 0UP
www.titanbooks.com

Find us on Facebook: www.facebook.com/TitanBooks
Follow us on X: @titanbooks

©2024 ZeniMax Media Inc. The Elder Scrolls Online developed by ZeniMax Online Studios LLC, a ZeniMax Media company. ZeniMax, The Elder Scrolls, Bethesda, Bethesda Softworks and related logos are registered trademarks or trademarks of ZeniMax Media Inc. in the US and/or other countries. All other trademarks and trade names are the property of their respective owners. All Rights Reserved.

Published by arrangement with Insight Editions, San Rafael, California, in 2024. www.insighteditions.com

No part of this publication may be reproduced, stored in a retrieval system, or transmitted, in any form or by any means without the prior written permission of the publisher, nor be otherwise circulated in any form of binding or cover other than that in which it is published and without a similar condition being imposed on the subsequent purchaser.

A CIP catalogue record for this title is available from the British Library.

ISBN: 9781803366098

Publisher: Raoul Goff
VP, Co-Publisher: Vanessa Lopez
VP, Creative: Chrissy Kwasnik
VP, Manufacturing: Alix Nicholaeff
VP, Group Managing Editor: Vicki Jaeger
Publishing Director: Mike Degler
Design Manager: Megan Sinead-Harris
Executive Editor: Jennifer Sims
Editor: Rick Chilot
Editorial Assistant: Sadie Lowry
Managing Editor: Maria Spano
Senior Production Editor: Michael Hylton
Senior Production Manager: Greg Steffen
Senior Production Manager, Subsidiary Rights: Lina s Palma-Temena

Text by Tori Schaeffer
Illustrations by Erika Hollice
Layout design by *tabula rasa* graphic design

Insight Editions, in association with Roots of Peace, will plant two trees for each tree used in the manufacturing of this book. Roots of Peace is an internationally renowned humanitarian organization dedicated to eradicating land mines worldwide and converting war-torn lands into productive farms and wildlife habitats. Roots of Peace will plant two million fruit and nut trees in Afghanistan and provide farmers there with the skills and support necessary for sustainable land use.

Manufactured in China by Insight Editions

10 9 8 7 6 5 4 3 2 1